You'll love this bo

A business owner who loves what you
around your neck.

Desperate to get out of the rut, increase sales, grow profits, reduce stress
levels and get your life back.

Looking for a step-by-step program to get you back on track, boost your
confidence and point you in the right direction.

Feeling alone.

Missing the money, profit, growth, free time, happy customers, fun and
laughter that are the rewards for becoming a Grown-Up Business.

Determined to build a business that is better in every way to your peers
and competitors.

Testimonials

"If you operate a business, buy this book today. Not tomorrow. Today."
Sam Carpenter - Author of Work the System: The Simple Mechanics of Making More and Working Less

"The perfect book for a small business owner who wants better but isn't sure how to make it happen."
Tim Levey - Author of Profit Improvement in a Week and Never Cut Costs

"This book is overflowing with useful ideas and strategies that would help a struggling or stagnant business blossom."
Jane Mallin

"Running a business for years can sometimes mean you operate in a groove. The Grown-Up Business helps you to creatively step out of the 'groove' to give you a new perspective on what's going on in your business and provides great strategies to reinvent or remodel the way you do things. One book to keep open on your desk!"
Trish Stretton - MD, People face2face Ltd

"Shirley's book is really helpful on two fronts, firstly it's an easy to read and understand book on business and secondly because it's so stuffed with ideas you can also use it as a work book as you follow step by step the key tasks identified in each chapter to help you make your business a success."
Laurence Ainsworth - Managing High Growth

Permissions

About Shirley Mansfield

Shirley Mansfield is an author, a high growth business coach, trainer and facilitator, and has a formidable reputation for being a master problem solver for businesses.

Shirley understands fully that owning and running a business can be a lonely place, however supportive your family might be. In the same way that sportsmen and women have coaches to help them to perform to the best of their ability, Shirley believes that every business owner should have access to expert business coaching to help them grow.

Shirley has worked in business, for businesses and with businesses for over 30 years; the last five as a high growth business coach. She has been a company director, non-executive director, functional director and holds the IOD Certificate in Company Direction, MCIM and ACII qualifications.

During a 20-year career in the City, Shirley worked in financial and professional services, with a number of FTSE 250s in marketing, change, sales, and re-engineering, as a problem solver and solution finder. Shirley also worked in heavy manufacturing, the charity sector and with several family businesses. Now she trains, coaches and mentors business owners who want to make more money, have more time, less stress, and more business success. Since setting up her own coaching practice *CoachSME*, she has helped businesses of all sizes achieve their true potential by helping them to overcome the obstacles in their path.

In her new book *The Grown-Up Business*, Shirley helps business owners and their companies truly come of age, build on their initial enthusiasm and put down the firm foundations necessary for sustained growth. Shirley lives in Kent with her husband Steve, and can be found in the garden or on the golf course, where she is still trying to reduce her 16 handicap, when not helping businesses become a Grown-Up Business.

The Grown-Up Business is dedicated to anyone who looks for and finds the best in people, gives them a pat on the back, boosts their confidence, and tells them they can, not they can't!

THE GROWN-UP BUSINESS

Shirley Mansfield

Published by Filament Publishing Ltd
16 Croydon Road, Waddon, Croydon, Surrey CR0 4PA, United Kingdom
Telephone +44 (0)20 8688 2598 | Fax +44 (0)20 7183 7186
info@filamentpublishing.com | www.filamentpublishing.com

This book is designed to provide information on how you can improve your business.

The purpose of this book is to inform and entertain the reader on the subject, drawing on many sources of information as well as personal experience. It is published for general reference and is not intended to be definitive guidance on your circumstances or as a substitute for independent verification by readers.

Although the author and publisher have made all reasonable efforts to ensure the accuracy and completeness of the information contained within, we cannot assume any responsibility for errors, inaccuracies, omissions, or inconsistencies or reliance on the same.

This book is sold on the understanding that neither the publisher nor the author are engaged in providing accounting, legal or other professional services. If legal and/or other expert assistance is required, the services of a competent professional should be sought.

Neither the author nor the publisher accept any liability, howsoever caused, to any person and/or entity in relation to any loss, damage or expense caused or incurred as a result of acting, or failing to act as a result of information contained in this book.

The right of Shirley Mansfield to be identified as the author of this work has been asserted by her in accordance with the Designs and Copyright Act 1988.

ISBN - 978-1-910125-58-8

Printed by CreateSpace

Table of Contents

Foreword

"If you operate a business, buy this book today. Not tomorrow. Today."

It's not often that I endorse a business book because the vast majority beat around the bush and wax too philosophical for my taste. But *Grown-Up* is different. It's honed in the non-theoretical/let's-face-reality world, and is down-and-dirty useful. It is my pleasure to make a strong endorsement.

I'm a systems-mindset, international business consultant specializing in fixing broken businesses and here's something that I know for sure: the fixing happens in the mechanics of an operation and that fixing can only begin at the very top, at the ownership level. Only there can permanent change begin to take place.

Another essential fact: a faux-business is one in which the owner insists on working inside, day and night, to make it work. *That's a job*, and usually a lousy job at that. A true business is one that stands alone; one that produces a profit – and provides jobs and a great product or service – as a self-contained entity that is separate from the owner. Anything less than this is a self-imposed job.

Shirley's book begins with the comparison of a business with a human life… It's a perfect analogy, really, and this thread weaves its way throughout.

Change? Change starts with a "tweak in the head," and that engenders a separation from the business, and that separation leads naturally to the point where problems are solved by "awareness, then analysis and then identification," and then, next… "reviewing, making a decision and prescribing." Well, it's very simple: one does this over and over and over again until one ends up with an "adult business." No more fire-killing and a great bottom line. This is a business that has a backbone, stands on its own, and creates value for all involved… and is worth tangible value to the owner as an independent money-making machine.

Grown-Up assertively addresses the emotional aspects of operating an enterprise. One has to stay motivated and this means the inevitable emotional slumps must be minimized and remain short-lived. How does one accomplish this? It's in these pages, with scores of actual real-world approaches and solutions. I really enjoyed this book!

And, another important thread that weaves its way throughout: "Tiny tweaks can have a massive impact." It's all about systemization and process control.

Grown-Up is more than a front-to-back read: It's a practical handbook in which one can dip in and out. It's a comfort to have on the night stand by the bed, and as a permanent passenger in the back seat of the car. For the struggling business owner - or the owner who's doing fine but just isn't advancing - *The Grown-Up Business* is mandatory reading.

Sam Carpenter, author of *Work the System: The Simple Mechanics of Making More and Working Less*
September, 2014

Preface

Congratulations. You own a business, you're running the company. You've driven it forward from its launch. You've made sales, employed people, made money (we hope), but it hasn't set the world on fire yet. Something just isn't right.

The great idea you had, the plan, and the bucket-load of passion, were all in place when you started out. You've worked hard, 24/7, to make it a reality. The business is doing okay, the company is busy, you're really busy, but you just don't seem to be making as much progress as you'd like to. Whatever you feel like at this moment, let me tell you that you're doing great. It might not be perfect, but with a little more focus, determination, planning, and organisation, I can help your business to grow up and make more money.

Your business's growth mirrors the growth of a person. In the birth of the business, you focus on survival first, just as one does with the birth of a child. Once you've mastered your business's survival, then you can turn your attention to making it thrive. Your business is probably in its Early Years now, so you're focusing on making the right decisions about where to take it. At this stage, it's easy to go round and round in circles. You're in discovery mode, but are unsure whether or not you've made the right discovery that will help you make the best decision. Growing your business from the Early Years of childhood into a Teenager means that your challenge is strategy. Crucially, your commitment will be tested time and time again – as with teenagers!

Continued growth through the Young Adult, Family, and Mature phases brings more challenges, but with a solid foundation in place these become easier to deal with effectively. You'll know when you reach Grown-Up Business status: your business has a momentum and rhythm about it that means customers always have a consistent, valuable experience, which in turn means they buy again and again. As this happens, you get more time, enthusiasm, and money to take advantage of an increasing number and variety of opportunities.

Running your own business can be tough, unrewarding, stressful, and downright time-consuming. Sometimes you feel as if you're working for the minimum wage! But when you transform your business into a Grown-Up Business, it's one of the best jobs in the world.

When you're wrestling with the next steps – *How can I grow, make more money and have time too?* – then you need some help. This is especially true when you're trying to decide which paths to choose, but never quite making a decision. Many business owners have been where you are now, but they didn't get any help. It's easier not to make any decisions. The business drifts; nothing is resolved, it has no direction, no focus, no reward…

What the majority of those business owners don't have, or aren't even aware that they need, is a toolkit of management skills. This has nothing to do with their technical competence or expertise. It's not about the area of their business; it's about the business itself. The essential skills in a business owner's toolkit are things like planning, problem solving, systematisation, and decision-making. If you don't learn and develop these skills, it will have serious consequences. You are your company.

Many of the business owners I work with recognise that they need some help to discover what they should be doing. I find that they aren't measuring themselves against the big boys like Ray Kroc, Jeff Bezos, or Lord Sugar, but against their friends, colleagues, or competitors, who started businesses at the same time as they did. If you're asking yourself the following questions, you need a little help to make your business better. How many of these questions sound familiar?

1 Why have they grown faster than us?
2 How did they expand more quickly than us?
3 How do they make more money than we do?
4 How can they afford to have a better car than me?
5 How have they taken so many holidays?

If you're asking yourself those questions, you need a little help to make your business better, because the answer to all those questions is, "They've grown up." They've become a Grown-Up Business. The single biggest element to their success over yours is working very hard on the important parts of their business. In Grown-Up Businesses, the owners know what they want to achieve, when, and how it will happen. They aren't wasting time, money, and energy firefighting the same problems every day. They focus on solving problems quickly and effectively so that they never have to solve them again. They continually make sure that the customer experience is consistently consistent and in line with the company's standards. They have time to generate or spot opportunities to make the business better.

It's time for a second "Congratulations!" You've found the Grown-Up Business book, which I wrote for business owners just like you. Whether you started your business from scratch, inherited or bought the company, or are the general manager, you're ready to learn how to make your business Grown-Up.

Why this book now?

You know that your business could be so much better – as good as that friend's who set up their company at the same time as you, but who seems to be doing a whole lot better! You're not happy with the business's performance and you've been trying to work out what's wrong, but you can't put your finger on it. You really don't want to fall out of love with it. You don't want it to become a chore or a millstone around your neck. You want to achieve the dream you had when you started. You want it to be fun again. You're not prepared to give up yet, even though you tell yourself that there must be easier ways to earn a living!

The really good business idea you had just needs some help to get a bit more organised and focused. Then you can be as good as, if not better, than your competitors and friends.

Why you?

You're tenacious. You're not ready to throw in the towel, but you recognise that there's a problem. You've probably tried to sort it out, possibly only scratching the surface. You think you know what to do, but… Doubt creeps in: *What if that's wrong, what do I do then, what will happen next?*

The fantastic news is that you're ready for help. You've been searching for a solution. You're open and receptive to learning what needs to happen, what your options are, and how to put the changes into practice.

This won't be easy. At times along the way, you'll feel like giving up. It'll take time; there's no magic wand. If you think you're working long hours now, you'll need to add a few more – but only for short while. Soon, you'll be freeing up lots of time for the important stuff.

Why me?

I'm a master problem solver. After a 20-year career in the City working on the merger of Lloyds and TSB, and a number of FTSE 250s in marketing, change, sales, and re-engineering, as a problem solver and solution finder, I started coaching. I train and mentor business owners who want to make more money and have more time, less stress, and more business success. I only work with the business owner: they have the loneliest job and they're the ones who really drive the change through the business. Hardly a day goes by without a breakthrough success with my clients. For business owners without that help and coaching, though, I know that they struggle to implement the step change they need. They…

- don't know what has to be done
- just never get around to doing it
- don't know how to do it
- don't have the confidence to take that scary step
- believe they're too busy to make the change

Instead, their days are filled with firefighting problem after problem and that's so depressing. That's when a business owner needs help.

I believe that companies that grow up make more money, have more choices, have more time to seek out exciting and profitable opportunities, reduce stress levels, and improve the well-being of everyone that the organisation touches.

What's it all about?

This book isn't just the theory: it's a how-to. It explains the what and the why, so you can understand the issue and learn how to tackle it. At the end of each section, you'll find exercises and tips that guarantee you can implement what you've learnt, step by step.

Chapter 1 Why You Need to Become a Grown-Up Business

I'll show you what a Grown-Up Business looks like and introduce you to the first steps to get you there. The leader of a Grown-Up Business also grows up and commits to new learning, not once but all the time. We'll look at my two golden rules for a successful business, the offering and the buyer, and at how important your original dreams, plans, and goals are to achieving success. Welcome to your journey.

Chapter 2 The Growing-Up Business Model

With the Growing-Up Business Model, we look at the growing-up steps from your business's birth until it reaches Grown-Up status. You'll find out how a business goes from survival mode, through the growing pains, to achieving momentum and maturity. Each stage – Birth, Early Years, Teenager, Young Adult, Family, and Maturity – has its own focus, which will guide you through the actions you need to take to get momentum in your business.

Chapter 3 Clear the Obstacles

Before you can move forward, you have to clear the obstacles. You are critical to your business's growth, so this entire chapter concentrates on what you have to do, how, and when. We'll deal with the challenges together: how to find the right mindset, how to give yourself permission for time off, when to do the important stuff, and how to reignite your dream, as well as the strategies that you can put in place to help you. If you want success, you can have it.

Chapter 4 Time to Get Some Help

It can be lonely running a business, even if you have lots of staff around you. There are five ways to get the help you need: a great boss, an accountable person, a brilliant support network, a bank of experts to pull in when needed, and your business networks. Sounding boards, intellectual challenge, and expert advisors are all part of the recipe.

Chapter 5 Set the Standards

Now it's time to focus on everything that you've let drift in your company – all the business-critical items that you've muddled along without, so far. Don't beat yourself up: with a little effort and a keen focus, you can put in place your manifesto, goals, standards, and work-house rules. And once you have, they'll have an immediate and positive impact on your business growth.

Chapter 6 Do Something Different and Make More Money

Doing the same thing over and over again only brings the same result. In this chapter, you'll learn the six areas where you can make vast improvements in your business. These will revolutionise how it operates and make you more money. You'll discover your moments of truth, the KISS principle, how to plug the gaps, why change is good, and how to use a pair of waste goggles. Making money has to be the goal and even tiny tweaks can have a massive impact.

Chapter 7 Reaching Maturity

As your business grows up, it changes. A rhythm starts to build and consistency improves. It's time to streamline the business and really start to scale up. Your focus now becomes processes, systematisation, finding a place for everything, and a customer-centric business. You'll embrace your new role and get used to smiling more!

Chapter 8 Know Your Numbers

In small businesses, we so often overlook the numbers: what are they telling you to do? Could you pitch to a Dragon at a minute's notice and win? Running a Grown-Up Business is all about knowing the numbers; numbers are critical. I'll show you why targets, variances, forecasts, projections, actual performance indicators, and management are a must for any Grown-Up Business – and how to get to grips with your numbers. You'll also learn how to create a Grown-Up Business forecast.

Chapter 9 Solve Problems, Permanently

Problems crop up everywhere, so you need to understand how to solve them effectively and permanently. If you don't solve the problem, it could kill your business. This chapter guides you through The Nine Essential Skills of Problem Solving. The first three tasks are to be aware, analyse, and identify. Next, you review, make a decision, and prescribe. Finally, you systematise, commit, and lead.

Chapter 10 Opportunity Knocks

Welcome to your new Grown-Up Business. It's running like a well-oiled machine. Is it time to sell it or to grow it even more? Opportunities will be landing in your lap: do you take advantage of them, or is it time to make your own opportunity?

Feel free to dip in and out of this book – it's a working document to be used as needed rather than read from cover to cover. The first two chapters are best read in order, then feel free to follow the book's order or dip into key chapters, whichever suits you best.

My goal is that everyone who picks up this book will learn how to turn their business into a Grown-Up Business with rhythm, momentum, and consistency, which in turn gives them more time and money to take advantage of the opportunities that are out there.

Throughout the chapters, there are lots of hints, tips, exercises, and templates, but not much room to write in this book or to make notes on the tablet! So I've created the Grown-Up Business workbooks for you, which you can download at www.grownupbusiness.com/extras.

Chapter 1

Why You Need to Become a Grown-Up Business

If you want a business that makes a positive difference to everyone it touches, that grows beyond its initial burst of enthusiasm, that is sustainable, scalable, and profitable, then you need to become a Grown-Up Business.

A Grown-Up Business is one that continually grows and refines its operations, its offering, and its income. It sells again and again to happy customers. It has a positive momentum; it's on an upward trajectory. As a business, it learns from the past but has its eyes firmly fixed on its future goals.

Let me say this right now: it's going to be tough. It's going to take your time, energy, and effort. It's going to test your mettle, but building a successful, sustainable Grown-Up Business is not a wild dream. You can turn it into a reality if you want to.

In this chapter, we're going to see what a Grown-Up Business looks like and discover the first steps that you'll need to take to get you there. The leader of a Grown-Up Business also grows up and commits to new learning – not once but all the time. You'll find out my two golden rules for a successful business and how important your original dreams, plans, and goals are important to achieving success. Welcome to your journey.

What does a Grown-Up Business look like?

We know when we're dealing with a Grown-Up Business. It's an enjoyable experience that we want to repeat over and over again. We feel valued, we're treated well, and everything runs smoothly without hiccups. Even though we're spending our hard-earned cash, we don't mind – we enjoy it. The staff that help us are smiling, attentive without being pushy. They want us to enjoy the experience and they want to please us. We also know what it's like to trade with a business that hasn't grown up.

Every Grown-Up Business has a set of attributes that sets it apart from the rest. Mastering these attributes doesn't guarantee success, but it does give you a better than average chance of developing a truly successful business. They are…

- marketing
- sales
- money
- people
- systems
- opportunity
- a great *you*!

A Grown-Up Business is well organised: it has a clear vision of what it wants and it has plans, goals, and targets. It's a great place to work: it has a higher than average staff retention rate and it employs really good people at every level. The products work every time. They deliver what the customer wants and needs. The customer service and aftercare behind the product is great. In fact, everything is under control and everything runs like clockwork. Each stage or process moves seamlessly on to the next. Everyone knows what to expect, what to do, and to what standard. Everything is *consistently* consistent.

When a business transitions into a Grown-Up Business it…

- charges more than its competitors
- understands its customers – probably better than they know themselves
- has a growing number of new and repeat customers, and those customers become their unpaid sales force
- sells more services and products
- always gets paid on time
- is systematised with robust processes and procedures
- becomes an expert purchaser of components, materials, and services
- is consistently consistent

Because of all of these factors, the business grows. It develops a consistency and rhythm to everything it does. This then builds momentum in the company and with that come great opportunities for the business to grow further.

Saga started 60 years ago in a small hotel in Folkestone and is now a successful, profitable, and Grown-Up Business. It employs over 24,000 people and has millions of very happy customers. It's so successful in supplying products and services to the over-50s that it effectively owns the over-50s market. With travel to worldwide destinations, cruise trips, hotels, insurance products, healthcare, home care, and its bestselling monthly magazine, Saga specialises in delivering exactly what its target market wants.

The De Haan family had a strong vision that has been the focus of everything they have done and will continue to do. They've kept growing because they've kept learning about their customers and the market. They continually improve everything about their business. They were one of the first companies to use direct mail back in the 60s. As they add new products and services, they systematically build the infrastructure that will enable them to repeat that service delivery every time.

Claridge's Hotel in London is another Grown-Up Business. It charges grown-up prices for the perfect guest experience. Nothing is left to chance: everything is checked and double-checked. They constantly seek out imperfections so they can refine and perfect their systems, and avoid disappointing their customers.

Whatever your views about McDonald's, it's definitely a Grown-Up Business. Whichever outlet you visit, the customer experience is exactly the same. It's highly systematised: every aspect of the business has a system that's been refined over time to make it foolproof and consistent. Absolutely everything has a process which is always followed to the letter. That's why it's almost impossible to have a burger without a gherkin! The business runs like a well-oiled machine, even when the boss isn't there. Everyone knows what to do, how to do it, and why they're doing it that way. The ability to build a Grown-Up Business like Ray Kroc did is the key to successful growth.

➲ Think about the businesses you've used over the past three months, including your own shopping.
    1 What did you like about the way they treated you?
    2 What didn't you like and why?
    3 Have you changed how you see them since the last time you had contact with them?

➲ Which company do you wish your company could emulate? What do you admire about them? What do they do that you want your company to do?

➲ Which of your competitors do you want to be better than?

Why did you start your business?

When you started your business, I'm sure you had a good idea of why you wanted to, and what you wanted to achieve. Most business owners think long and hard before setting up their company. They have plans, goals, passion, and a drive to start a business and succeed. Whatever your trigger was, I'm sure you created a clear picture in your mind of what it would be like running your own company and the success you'd have.

What is your reality today? Is it what you thought it was going to be? Instead of building that picture of success, has your vision ended up as a millstone around your neck, a chore instead of a pleasure, stressful instead of fun, standing still treading water instead of growing your income and profit?

Let's take a look at how your initial dreams for your business can become your reality, and how to regain that enthusiasm if you've lost it along the way.

The owners of successful Grown-Up Businesses have a crystal-clear vision of everything that the business should be: how it operates, the products, who the customers are and how they are treated, the standards, the systems, and the success. They start working on the business with the end vision in mind. They see this vision as the reality they can attain, even though they know it's going to be hard work. That vision, that dream, is essential when the going gets tough. Being able to keep their total focus on the dream during the dark days is what helps them succeed.

Any successful sports person will tell you about the constant training and practice, the early starts, the doubts, the sacrifices, the injuries, the problems, and the knockbacks that all happened for years before they tasted even a little success. Those knockbacks and their ability to overcome them transformed them into the successful sports people they became. If you've never made a mistake or had a knockback, then you've never learnt.

I've yet to find a successful business owner who hasn't failed at something. When you're facing failure, dealing with a mistake, overcoming yet another problem, it's your strong vision and goal that keeps you going. If you lose sight of your dream, or it becomes cloudy, you'll find it virtually impossible to climb out of that depressive state. If your reality is now a long way away from your dream, you've lost your way. Now is the very best time to remind yourself why you started your company in the first place. Getting back in touch with your dream is an excellent motivator: it will give you an energy boost to get you back on track.

Your team will soon know when you've remembered your dream. They'll see you change into the leader you want to be as your passion, drive, and focus returns. And they'll respond. They'll match your positive mood and then your customers will see that positive difference too.

Jo had trained as a bookkeeper and whilst her three children were very young, she freelanced from home, but she always wanted more. She dreamt of a successful business with herself at the helm to guide and direct it, like a ship steaming towards its destination.

But she wasn't earning much, even though she was putting in the work. Her clients were delighted with her service and she worried that if she put her prices up, her customers would go elsewhere – so she didn't. To make more money, she just added more clients and worked even more hours. Time off was impossible; her clients needed her. As she improved and got faster, she didn't earn more, because she charged by the hour when she should have been charging for her expertise and the value that she delivered.

She was stuck in the classic struggle between working in the business and working on it. She didn't have time to plan, because she was working too hard. As any good business person will tell you, failing to plan is planning to fail.

Jo had the technical skills and continued to gain more qualifications as she looked after her happy clients from home. She knew other bookkeepers too and quickly recognised that although they were technically good, they weren't good at finding new clients. Jo was and her clients were referring other clients to her. She also built a strong relationship with a local accountancy firm, who referred even more clients. She was bursting at the seams.

When her second child went to school, she launched The Bookkeeping Company. That's when I met Jo and she told me her dreams:

- to build a successful, growing, and well-respected bookkeeping practice
- to provide a beautiful home for her family (She had a lovely vision of Christmas dinner with every member of her family around the same table.)
- to help and support stay-at-home mums to return to the workplace with a fulfilling job
- to be recognised as an expert in her field
- to provide exceptional, professional bookkeeping services to even more clients

18 months later, Jo had a team of 15 staff all working flexible hours between 7 am and 10 pm, and a bank of happy clients. She had launched a new payroll service too. The Institute of Certified Bookkeepers recognised her success, making her a finalist in the Practice of the Year awards. What a fantastic start! Jo still has lots to achieve and she continues to work towards her dreams, which now include opening a series of offices.

➲ Now put the book down, grab a cup of tea or a glass of something, and close your eyes. Think back to the day you set up your company. What was your dream, your plan, or your goal? Remind yourself why you started your company.

➲ Write down your dream – use bullet points (it's quicker) and include anything and everything about it.

➲ Now turn your attention to your current reality. What has your dream turned into? Use your list to tick or cross what is and isn't working.

My two golden rules for any business

Anyone can start a business, but how do you make it work, survive, and then thrive? There are two golden rules for any business. First, you must have a product or service offering that does what it should do. That means that it works; it solves a client's problem. It's reliable and functional. Remember the man who sold the bomb detectors that didn't work? He ended up in prison! Second, there must be people who want what you have and are willing to pay you money for it. If it works but no one wants it, you don't have a business.

If you have both these things, a product that works and people who want it, then every problem and challenge can be overcome. Without these two things in place, you will fail. So if you're thinking about starting a business, you have to get a big "yes" to both of these rules. Let's review why these rules are so critical to your business success.

The product must work

If the product or service doesn't do the job or isn't up to scratch, you might make a few sales but you'll never get repeat sales. You'll always be looking for new and unsuspecting customers to buy your subpar product or service.

Frances makes and sells Clipper NoteBooks, and they work. The notebooks come with lovely paper and the book cover has pockets to securely store clippings, cards, and scraps of paper. It has a fastener to keep everything together. A standard notebook has clippings slipped between the pages, but pick it up the wrong way and everything falls to the floor. The Clipper NoteBook is successful, because it works.

It's time to take a long hard look at your products and services. Do they work? Assess your entire range: be critical but fair. Since you started your business, you'll have added new options, but probably overlooked the old ones you still had.

Car manufacturers are skilled in product improvement and they know that the majority of customers will be attracted by an improved product. They're equally good at running down stocks of old products, though, before the replacement is launched.

If you have a better offering than before, then clear out the old ones now. Not only will you reduce complexity, you'll increase cash and be able to focus on supplying the best that you can.

People must want it

Do people want it? To answer this, we must know what needs and wants your product or service satisfies. Does it solve a problem for a specific sector of the market? If so, how does it solve that problem and who needs your solution? If it's a brand-new product, how will you let people know about a product they might not even be looking for? If it doesn't solve a problem or satisfy a desire, it's time to go back to the drawing board. People must want what you have to offer.

I've had start-ups approach me for help who've told me, "There isn't anything like this on the market, we don't have any competitors, so we're onto a winner!" If you're in this situation, you need to ask yourself why there isn't anything like it on the market. Is it because no one actually wants or needs it? Two of these optimistic start-ups hadn't carried out market research with any potential customers. When they did, neither business launched.

Once you're sure you have a "YES" product, you need to think about who is going to buy it from you. If your prospective customers are buying a similar product from competitors, ask yourself, "Why would they buy from me?" What's different about you? That might include…

- a better product
- quicker delivery
- cheaper parts and accessories
- better availability
- fantastic customer service and aftercare
- flexible pricing

Remember, your competitors aren't just the companies selling the same product as you. Imagine you ran a restaurant. Your immediate competitors would be other restaurants, yes, but also home cooking, supermarket dinner-for-two deals, the savings accounts or the holiday fund, theatre, cinema, or other activities.

Identifying who will want it is all about customer segmentation or your target market. How do you discover who the right customers are and where you find them? You need to develop a very clear picture in your mind of your customer and hold it in your head. Now you can focus everything that your company does as if you were dealing with this model customer.

If you trade directly with the public, think about some of these characteristics when you're building a picture of your ideal customer:

- their income level, profession, or the type of work they do
- what type of property they own or live in
- what car they drive
- which supermarket and shops they use, or whether they're internet buyers
- their marital status, age, and gender
- their hobbies, interests, holiday destinations

If you supply other businesses, consider these aspects:

- type of business
- size: turnover and/or employee numbers
- location
- ability to pay and credit worthiness
- green credentials
- who makes the buying decision

Having that picture of your customer is essential, but you can't stop here. To answer the second question fully, you absolutely have to find out whether or not your target customer will actually buy from you. Time to do some market research!

John launched his company last year. He planned to sell a service to micro and small businesses, whereby they could outsource anything that the business owner couldn't or didn't want to do for a monthly fee. John wasn't going to be a virtual assistant – he would be the middle man. He'd find customers who needed help and then he'd outsource the work to a team of home workers, bookkeepers, and specialists such as lawyers and accountants. He would take a margin.

The problem was that no one wanted his services. If they needed a bookkeeper, lawyer, project manager, or another specialist, they found one themselves. John's target customers wanted to find their own specialist suppliers or do it themselves. They didn't want the middleman service that John was offering, so they didn't buy it. John worked really hard to build the business, until he finally realised that it would never work: no one wanted what he had to offer.

Part of the process in developing a product or service is to find out exactly what customers want, not to second-guess them. Talk to them: ask questions and find out what they want before you rack up development and launch costs only to find your shelves stocked with products that no one wants. Grown-Up Businesses make sure they have buyers for new products, even before they start manufacturing, and certainly before the launch date. Apple is great at this: the news programmes regularly cover the long queues on the launch days for its new products. Successful training companies take time to understand precisely what delegates want before they develop and launch a new training course. This means they keep the products range as simple as possible, but effective and profitable. They don't waste development costs and time on products and services that are too complex for customers or for them to deliver.

➲ What needs and wants does your product or service satisfy? What problem are you solving or what pleasure are you giving?

➲ Search out product and services that are in the same or a similar category to yours.

➲ Make a list of your product's key features and then rank it alongside your competitors'. I use a scale of 1 to 5 where 1 is "worse than" and 5 is "better than". Once you complete this exercise, you'll know if your products are in demand.

➲ Draw up a detailed profile of your ideal client or customer.

➲ Now take your product or service and talk to a selection of your target customers to find out whether or not they would buy the product and if so whether they'd buy from you.

Commit to new learning and succeed

Developing a Grown-Up Business takes hard work – lots of it. It requires you to lead the way. You're the only person that can take your company on this journey, so reinforcing your original vision and goals, or your new dream, is vital. Starting is easy; maintaining total commitment through thick and thin is what makes the difference between mediocre or meteoric success. You must also commit to learning every day. As well as learning new business skills, you'll have to continually learn about your business, your market, your customers and your competitors.

If you're going to help your business grow up, you have to learn new skills, but that doesn't necessarily mean signing up for a bunch of courses. Very little of our learning takes place in a classroom: most of our skills are developed and honed elsewhere. Books like this one help you learn something new, different, or innovative. Every time you talk to someone else, you have the chance to learn something new. Reliable websites can be a great reference book as you learn on the job. How you learn varies according to your personality, your own learning style, and whether you're working on technical or soft skills to learn. You also need to learn a lot about your business.

Technical skills

Technical knowledge and skills include finance, marketing, planning, strategy, operations, IT, HR, and so on. Don't worry, you won't have to become qualified in all of these fields; you just have to understand them well enough. How will you hire a great marketer if you don't know the subject? What will you do when your accountant gives you the monthly or annual figures; will you know what they're telling you? You have to understand all of these aspects if you're going to start asking the right questions of your business. You'll be hiring people (internal and external) to do the work, but you will be directing it, so it's time to brush up your knowledge and learn more.

Leadership skills

The soft skills centre on how you behave and communicate – the leadership skills. Improving your leadership skills will help you get the best out of the people that you work with, from staff and customers to suppliers and stakeholders. Most business leaders don't spend enough time recognising their own attributes or how competent they are at these leadership skills. Without any self-assessment, it's hard to know where to direct your efforts to improve your skills. In the end, many simply ignore these skills and continue to muddle along, never getting the best out of people.

I believe that a leader should be…

- authentic
- consistent
- adaptable
- generous
- empowering
- convicted
- above all, a great communicator

You need to build a great team around you, developing the culture, telling the story, and taking people with you. You need to be a motivator, supporter, director, and disciplinarian, and take responsibility for them too. You need to maintain your composure at all times, be resourceful and creative, and keep up standards as well. That's all on top of being a good negotiator, influencer, decision-maker and problem solver! Master these skills and talented people will want to work for you.

Learning about your business

As a business owner, you are most likely a director of a limited company. This means you have a legal requirement to run the business correctly. To do that, you have to learn continually what's going on in your business and understand how you are trading. Apart from the legal responsibility, you also have a moral responsibility to your shareholders, customers, and staff to make sure that the business is running correctly. You can only do this if you're always learning about your customers, your market, your environment and legal responsibilities, economics, money, people, marketing, and sales. You absolutely have to know everything about your business.

Your skill set is about to change and grow. You'll need to learn about…

- marketing and sales
- finance and numbers
- production, workflow, and resource planning
- organisation
- developing and implementing processes
- planning and visioning
- risk management
- people
- SHE (safety, health and environment)

Knowing your business inside out, what markets you operate in, and who does and doesn't buy your products is a good place to start. What do you and don't you know about your company and its immediate market opportunity? Explore what's happening in the wider world and in other industries, too: learn what you can import into your company.

I'm surprised at how little some business owners know about their own business. If you don't know what's happening, how do you know if it's working to maximum effectiveness or what you need to improve? You can't.

Like many others, I often watch *Dragons' Den*. Although it's made for television entertainment rather than as an educational programme, it's a great learning tool. I always learn something from the Dragons' interrogation – mostly what the wrong answers are! I cringe when the Dragons start questioning the pitcher about their business, their markets, and the size of their business opportunity. Knowing the numbers always separates the best from the also-rans.

Sadly, so few business owners have taken the time to really learn, remember, and understand their business or the market opportunity. The market research seems to have eluded most of them. They haven't asked the questions who, what, why, where, when and how. These six questions are the only ones we need. They're the questions that the Dragons are asking!

⮎ Imagine that you're going to pitch for £100,000 investment on *Dragons' Den*. You'll have to prove to the Dragons that you know your company and market inside out. Try these questions. Can you answer them fully without having to look it up?

1 How many units have you sold in the past three months?
2 What percentage of your customers buys again?
3 What is your average order value?
4 What do your competitors do that you don't?
5 What is your gross profit percentage and number?
6 Why do your customers buy from you?
7 What will your numbers be in three years' time and why?

You can't ignore the problem, you have to solve it now

We all recognise that our companies could do better – we're not running smoothly or not able to grasp business opportunities with both hands. We spend too much time dealing with the same problem over and over again.

Grown-Up Businesses are excellent at solving problems. They don't subscribe to the head-in-the-sand mentality. They don't accept phrases like "I'll ignore it and it'll go away" or "I'll do that later" or "It's not my problem". Instead they embrace a problem. They know it's important to deal with problems as they arise and not allow them to fester or grow. They know that problems cost the business lots of money. Having to deal with the same problem over and over again is just so depressing. Solving the problem now – and I mean really solving the problem, once and for all – transforms a business's profitability, success, longevity, and its overall happiness.

When a problem crops up, it's an opportunity to make your business better, quicker, stronger, or faster. Ignoring a problem, an issue, or an obstacle delays or stops you concentrating on business opportunities. It wastes company time and money. Extremely Grown-Up Businesses not only solve problems, they go looking for them. They have their eyes peeled all day, every day, in search of problems within their company. They get on and solve the problem, then they move on to the next one and solve that too. Soon they're seeing massive improvements. Once you start solving problems, you save time and money. You'll notice the difference and so will your team and your customers.

ABC Ltd is a web design agency specialising in websites, apps, and mobile solutions for the sporting industry. Their target market is everything and everyone from sports associations to clubs and sporting celebrities. They were constantly selling, as they had to maintain a strong pipeline of potential sales to convert into paid work. They needed a new sales director and when someone approached them for a job in sales, they saved the recruitment fee and employed him.

It soon became clear that he was the wrong person for the role. The sales pipeline started to stagnate, new enquiries dried up, and the future income stream for ABC Ltd weakened. Days and weeks went by. The senior management team kept hoping that the situation would improve, but it didn't. In the end, the management team moved into the sales department to help with the sales effort – all in addition to their own day jobs. Sales improved, but the sales director remained in post. Soon after the management team returned to their day jobs, sales slipped back again and the senior management had to rescue the situation once again. Still, the sales director remained. He was an expensive resource with a hefty expense account too. By now his team of account managers had lost faith in him and the business started on a downward spiral. Why was he still there? He had too thick a skin to resign, but why weren't the management team dealing with the problem?

The senior management team certainly talked a lot about the sales director's poor performance – they spent ages at every management meeting discussing it, but they didn't take any action until it was almost too late.

They lost out massively. Not only were they paying for a non-effective sales director but they also lost the opportunity to recruit somebody better and probably for less money. The business suffered redundancies in the web development and studio team. The business almost failed and finally the sales director was fired.

By then, the financial cushion was very thin and once again the management team had to take over sales. They saved the sales director's overhead and salary and sales picked up, but it took time to recruit a new, more skilled sales director. Failing to solve the problem as soon as it was apparent was nearly fatal for ABC Ltd. The impact on the business was dramatic.

There will be times when you have to make a tough or unpleasant decision that solves the problem. None of us enjoy these tasks, but the penalty for not solving the problem can be fatal.

Your business might be okay for now but it's not good enough for the future. Are you ready to make changes so that your business can start to give you more of what you want? Being ready to grow up is the foundation of this book.

If you don't think that you or your business has any problems, then you may be in denial. You can *always* learn something new and there is always room for improvement. Only when my clients really want to change and improve can I help them. I'm here to help you, but you have to help yourself. So let's take a look at your business as it is today.

➲ The following questions are an initial assessment for you. Mark yourself out of 10 for each of the eight questions.

1 How well is your business growing?
2 How well are you supported, by your team and by your own advisors?
3 How clear are the guidelines for your business – customer service standards, team values and behaviours, and brand statement?
4 According to your cash flow forecast, how healthy does the next three months' trading look? How often do you review how your business operates, where you could make changes to either save or make more money?
5 How effective are the processes and systems in your business? Do they run smoothly and are they written down? When did you last review or improve them?
6 How often do you review your targets, business forecast, and performance? Do you have a current forecast in place?
7 How many problems have you dealt with this week – did you solve them permanently or will they pop up again?

8 How often do you want to kick yourself because you let a great opportunity slip through your fingers?

➲ Put your scores onto the chart below and join the scores together to look like a spiderweb. I imagine that your spider chart is a bit wonky, as some areas will be better than others. That means you can see which parts to concentrate on first.

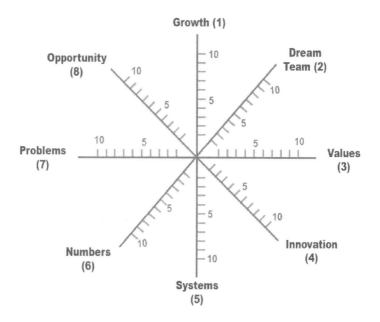

Grown-Up Businesses are successful. They make lots of money and customers flock to them and buy over and over again. They build momentum because they supply a consistent product, service, and customer experience every time, without exception. They solve problems even before they arise. They work continually to make the business better, quicker, stronger, faster, and more profitable. They have great relationships with their staff, customers, suppliers, and the community. Everyone has a clear vision of what success will look like and the person at the top keeps everyone focused on the end goal every day. That's the kind of business yours is going to be.

Chapter 2

The Growing-Up Business Model

Grown-Up Businesses have a momentum about them – a rhythm to everything they do. It's hard to get there, but when you do, life can deliver a whole pile of opportunities right to your doorstep.

Your working week probably stretches to seven days a week. You're at your desk with an enormous to-do list; you have customers wanting your attention and staff requiring direction, instruction, advice, or help; you have bills to pay, the phone ringing, e-mails pinging into your inbox, and not a minute to think! You're working hard and at the end of the day you're worn out. The prospect of doing it all again tomorrow just doesn't bear thinking about.

How many golden opportunities to grow or expand your business have passed you by because your nose was firmly attached to the grindstone? Has "I'm too busy" meant opportunities have slipped through your fingers? You didn't have the chance or the time to take advantage of the opportunity. If you had, you might have rushed headlong into the wrong decision – the impact could have been dramatic, even devastating. You want to be able to take those golden opportunities, but you need the time to evaluate them first. You need a measured approach. You need to climb each rung of the ladder in turn. If you try to miss out some rungs, you'll lose your footing and tumble down to the bottom only to have to start again.

In this chapter, we're going to look at the growing-up steps, from the birth of your business until it reaches Grown-Up status. Each stage – Birth, Early Years, Teenager, Young Adult, Family, and Maturity – has a specific focus. We'll look at the actions you need to take to achieve momentum. Then you can grasp the business opportunities by the scruff of the neck and take advantage of them!

The Growing-Up business model

You have to know where you are before you can plan the journey. You also need to know where you're going. Imagine being lost in a big city: how do you know which way to go to get home? Conversely, how do you decide how to get somewhere if you don't know where you're going?

The Growing-Up business model will help you do both. As you move through this chapter, you'll begin to understand where you are, where you have to get to, the route you have to take, and what you need to do at each stage. Each business moves from the bottom to the top. And yes, you're going to have to do some climbing.

The Growing-Up business model

Stage	Mode	Focus	Growth %	Fun Index
Mature	Momentum	Opportunity	64	☺☺☺
Family	Direction	Leadership	32	☺☺
Young Adult	Activity	Implementation	16	☺
Teenager	Strategy	Commitment	8	☺
Early Years	Decision	Discovery	4	☹
Birth	Survival	Measurement	0	☹☹
Pregnancy	Research	Planning	0	☹☹☹

As we grow up, we learn lots of different things. Some we think are useful, some not; some things we love, others we don't; some come easy, others are harder to learn, but learn we do. In the same way, as our companies grow up, we learn, refine, perfect and repeat the best bits, discard the bad bits. Our aim is to create a well-oiled machine that delivers consistent products and services to people who value what we supply, so that we can take advantage of the opportunities that arise to wow even more customers and make more money.

The first stage in every business is its birth – its first stage of life. Sadly, early mortality is the outcome for too many young companies. They didn't learn how to grow up. It's hard to have a wise head on young shoulders: just as we learn to read and write, we must learn how to run a business. It doesn't just come naturally. Even if your hobby is your business, you still have to *learn* how to run it.

The Clipper NoteBook Company – case study

Frances had an idea. She loved writing and her pleasure increased using a beautifully smooth pen and lovely writing paper – not the cheap stuff that acts like blotting paper! She was also a great clipper, clipping articles from magazines, recipes, business cards, leaflets, and bits of paper, but they were always falling out of her notebook. She also liked distinctive and unique products.

Pregnancy

Frances conceived the idea of The Clipper NoteBook Company: a fabric-covered notebook with slots and pockets inside both covers, beautiful paper, and a fastener so that nothing fell out. The product worked, but who would want them? She developed several designs and gave them to friends and family. Everyone loved them, but could she sell them? Would anyone buy them?

She made a batch, tucked them under her arm, and hit the street. She went to her club, to friends, to work colleagues, and asked lots of questions. She shopped until she dropped, seeing what was available on the market – the pricing, quality, and functionality. She had found a niche for handmade quality clipper notebooks and her company was born.

Birth

Now she had to make it work: the company was born and she entered Survival mode. She measured everything; components, materials, pricing, fashion trends, sales by size and colour, enquiries, web hits, everything. She engaged her clients to help her refine her designs. She collected feedback avidly and set up a mailing list, a wish list, a gift packaging service, and refills for her customers. She learnt lots, she changed a lot, and she started to set up systems. Every change helped refined her processes and systems.

Early Years

As she moved into the Early-Years stage, she made discoveries about every aspect of her company. She set the standards for The Clipper NoteBook Company – the quality and the range of products. She discovered how often people bought, how they bought, and how many purchases were gifts. She discovered how to buy components better and refine her manufacturing to make savings. Her brand developed and was consistent, positioning her right in the yummy-mummy and gift market. She identified key selling dates – a huge peak before Mother's Day and Christmas and a bump-up at Valentine's Day.

Teenager

The company was starting to grow up. Frances had built sales traction. She was working hard making the products with the help of friends and family, whilst trying to build the business. It was decision time: remain a lifestyle business or grow The Clipper NoteBook Company into a bigger, more successful company? Customers loved her products and she was feeling good. She decided she wanted to share her products with as many people as possible. It could work, but what next?

She needed a strategy: how was the baby going to grow into a Teenager, a real business? She had a picture in her mind of what she wanted. She had a clear vision of her notebooks in handbags, satchels, and briefcases, sitting on desks everywhere. She knew her customers and what they liked about the product and the brand. She knew the quality and standards she wanted. But she couldn't do it all alone. It was time to get some help.

She gathered some people together: her mentor, accountant, bank manager, and a marketing friend. They helped and she wrote her plan, nice and short, just the key points and no waffle: to manufacture unique clipper notebook covers in the UK to sell direct via her website to independent retailers, and to secure contracts with two major department stores and four online outlets within two years. Later on, she would extend the range to include diaries, e-readers, and iPad covers.

She also wrote down her challenges: sourcing the right products, designing new products, quality manufacturing, logistics, building the brand and a following, and the shortcomings in her own skill set. With her team, she finalised the three-year strategy, put cash flow forecasts in place, and devised the marketing calendar. She was ready to commit.

Young Adult

Having committed to her strategy, Frances moved into the implementation and activity stage. As the owner of a Young-Adult business, she couldn't let go of the reins – the business might spin out of her control. Her commitment was total. She built her systems and processes, making them robust enough that she could delegate, but not abdicate, responsibility.

She built a great team around her, from employed staff and outsourced workers to her advisory team, suppliers, and external network. Activity notched upwards; she managed, tracked, refined and delegated each new implementation to her growing team.

She put a performance dashboard in place to track what was happening, an early-warning system to highlight any problem areas. Her reforecasting cycle quickened as growth started accelerating. She had to understand the implications of a big order being placed: could they cope? Would the finances cover the outlay? It had to be managed all the way through, from purchasing materials to making sure quality remained high and customers received their deliveries on time.

Family

As The Clipper NoteBook Company moved into the Family stage, it had direction: it knew where it was going and why. Frances transitioned into a leader. She no longer made the product but oversaw her designs through the manufacturing and sales processes. Her focus was firmly on leading the company: revisiting strategy and tactics, either pulling the business back into line or taking part of it in a new direction.

Frances's team had grown. Recruiting the right people early on, those who "got the brand" and her vision, helped. Turnover was growing rapidly with new orders won and big contracts signed. The company was not yet a household name, but within its niche was well-known and respected. The products always had great reviews. Any issues that cropped up were swiftly dealt with and the customers wowed by her response. The website, her global shop front, attracted customers from

France, USA, and the Far East. Frances was great at communicating her vision and her leadership focus meant that the business continued in the right direction.

Maturity

The hard work Frances put in to building a solid foundation for her company and her steady measured approach to growing it resulted in a successful, mature company: it reached Maturity. Finding the momentum in the business ensured consistency in everything that the business did. With momentum come opportunities. Frances not only looked for new opportunities, such as export, she was also approached with numerous offers. Having set in place the right systems for the company to run smoothly, she was able to devote quality time to considering whether those opportunities were right for The Clipper NoteBook Company.

Growing a business from its Birth to its Maturity means that you have to grow too. And that means you have to keep asking questions, learning new skills, having insights, and making mistakes and learning from them.

➲ Using my Growing-Up Business model, locate yourself at one stage – the one where you really are, not the one where you'd like to be. It's okay to straddle two stages. Be truthful; otherwise this won't work. If you're considering starting a business, you'll be at the pregnancy stage. Whichever stage you're at, work from that basis as you read the rest of the chapter.

Step-by-step approach to growth

Throughout your personal life, you've faced challenges and new experiences, learnt new skills and perfected them. Then you moved onto the next growing-up stage. The principle of your business journey is no different. Whatever age you are, you've already grown up through some of these levels. You might be a young adult still trying to perfect the transition from teenager whilst you have your eye on being a family person. Wherever you are, that age brings with it a specific focus. It's the same with your business.

It's time to bring the model to life in your business. Use it as a framework to help you organise your thoughts – to stimulate your thinking with questions and to record insightful thinking in an easy format. This growth development method is your route map to success! It gives you the route to follow and you take it one step at a time. It's designed as a ladder. You start at the bottom, test the rung, and if it's solid, climb up. If not, stay there for a while and strengthen that rung before you move on. If there are weak rungs on the ladder, they will soon break and back you'll fall. At each stage, learn, improve, perfect, succeed, and then move up to the next level. As you climb through the levels from the bottom to the top, your business will develop, grow, and become more profitable.

It's really hard to jump from bottom to top in one leap: it occasionally works, but usually not. A much better method is a measured and steady progression through each step. By learning small chunks of skills, practising and perfecting them before taking the test, you have more chance of being successful. You focus on perfecting a skill so much that it becomes second nature. What a boost to your confidence when you pass a level and can start on the next one!

Locate your growth stage

Each level has a mode that defines what stage the business is at. When you launch your business, you're starting at the birth level: it's Survival mode. Now you can start moving through the growth phases until the Maturity mode, which is Momentum.

Don't try to make the leap from Birth to Maturity in one go – we all have to learn to walk before we can run! That said, you don't have to concentrate on just one level at a time: keeping an eye on one level up and one down is a good way to manage the progression. So if you're at the Teenager level, for example, your mode is Strategy and your focus is Commitment, but you'll also be thinking about the level above and below:

Stage	Mode	Focus	Growth %	Fun Index
Young Adult	Activity	Implementation	16	☺
Teenager	Strategy	Commitment	8	☺
Early Years	Decision	Discovery	4	☹

As you start to work on Strategy, you'll be fully embedding the Early Years mode of Decision. You'll also be starting to think about Young Adult mode of Activity.

You can move through the levels reasonably quickly, but if you skip over or are sloppy at completing the things you need to do at each level, you'll pay the price later on. Don't dwell at each stage for ages, but do a proper job at each stage: no half measures.

Locating the correct place on the model to start from is important. Strike too high up, and you'll have to go back down again. Strike too low, and you're letting your business stagnate.

Find your focus

While each Mode of the Growing-Up Business model defines what you'll achieve, the Focus indicates where your attention should be. This must be at the top of your to-do list, the first item on your job description. It is that critical to your success. Don't let this languish on the "I'll do it later" pile.

Look again at the Teenager stage as an example. Here, the Mode is Strategy and the Focus is Commitment. Deciding on a strategy should be relatively easy, but committing to delivering it must be your priority. 100% of the time, all day every day, commitment will be your focus. If you let your commitment waiver, you give your team permission to waiver as well, then you're back at square one. The same applies at Family level: the Mode is Direction and the Focus is Leadership. As a leader, your words and actions are visible every day. You need 100% focus. Any good leader will tell you that you have to learn new leadership skills, practise them, and make them your focus every day.

As you complete each level, you will have learnt new skills. Don't forget them as you start to develop the skills at the next stage. Take your learning with you, just as you have all your life.

Measure your growth

The Growing-Up business model is all about growing your business, so I use percentage growth as a measure for my clients. It would be tempting to put a monetary value on this model, but diverse companies have diverse starting points and your percentage increase will depend on where you start. The key point here is that growth accelerates as you build towards momentum.

There are several ways to set your growth measures:

1   Take last year's numbers and arbitrarily add a fixed % increase to all sales. So, for example…

Last year's sales (Money in)	£100,000
Last year's costs (Money Out)	£80,000
Add 10% to both money in and money out	£110,000 and £88,000

2   Set your end goal and work backwards in stages to assign a growth target. If you want to achieve sales of £500,000 in three years' time, then fix that figure and work backwards to give you the targets in years one and two. So if last year's sales were £100,000, you might then fix sales targets at £200,000 for year one, £350,000 for year two and £500,000 in year three. Your growth targets are + 100% in year one, +75% in year two and + 42% in the year three.

3   Use your rolling three-month figures (the last three months' figures added together and averaged) and add a fixed percentage. So sales in the last three months were £10,000, £12,000 and £14,000, then the average (£10,000 + £12,000 + £14,000 = £36,000 ÷ 3 = £13,000) is £13,000. You can add 10% making a new monthly target of £14,300 or quarterly target of £42,900.

4   Project on past actuals. Extend your current trajectory to see where you would get to if nothing changed and then add a forecast line to get you to where you want to be.

As you progress through the growing up stages, your growth will accelerate. The higher up the ladder you start, the more acceleration you get.

Include a fun index

Far too many of the business owners I meet tell me the fun has gone out of running a business. That's hardly surprising, following such a long recession, but life's too short not to have some fun. Survival mode is no fun and if you've been there you'll know: stress, long hours, little or no monetary reward, illness, divorce, and not even a smile. You can get out of Survival mode, though, and as you move up the ladder, you'll find fewer grimaces and more smiles. Moving up will bring more fun, reward, success, satisfaction, peace and pleasure.

Not everyone wants to be the biggest or the best company. I know from my work with hundreds of business owners that they want a fulfilling business life, not a boring, unrewarding treadmill. They don't want the business to run them anymore. They want to be proud of their company, to achieve, to have happy clients and employees, they want to have fun and reap the rewards of their hard work. Building a Grown-Up Business will give you choices; you can choose where you want to go.

Growing up, finding a rhythm, developing consistency in the company so that momentum builds all leads to new opportunities. So let's start your journey to becoming a Grown-Up Business.

➲ Now that you know where you are you can determine where you want to be on the model. Put your own growth percentages into the growth column.

Chapter 3

Clear the Obstacles

If a business is to grow, it must find the right attitude. As the business owner, leader, or manager, your attitude is crucial. What you say and do will either engage your teams and customers or not. Before embarking on this journey, you need to clear the obstacles, to know what you are up against. Most of what you're up against is, of course, you. You'll need to have passion, capability, drive, a thick skin, and the right mindset.

Because you're crucial to your businesses growth, this entire chapter concentrates on you and what you need to do. I'll highlight the challenges and show you how to find the right mindset, how to give yourself permission for time off and the time to do the important stuff, and how to reignite your dream. We'll also look at strategies that you can put in place to help you. If you want success, you can have it.

Find a positive mindset

Business advisors, consultants, and gurus throw around phrases such as "The £10M Mindset" and they're dreaming up fancy new phrases every day. Never mind what they're calling it now: the keyword is *mindset*. Mindset is all about getting your head in the right place: a clear vision, a positive outlook, being determined and committed, especially when everybody is telling you that "That won't work," or "You can't." The nasty surprises, failures, mistakes, the "It just won't go right" days are the ones that will really test your mettle – be strong and keep your positive mindset.

Grown-Up Businesses have been through the dark days. The difference is that they quickly get back on track and into the right mindset. If you want something badly enough, you'll find the right mindset: the attitude, determination and commitment will all be there. During the dark days, you'll need to give yourself a good talking-to and rediscover your positive mindset, fast! Only you can drive your business's growth. You're the boss, the leader, the driving force of the business. It's a big commitment and a responsibility that will sometimes sit heavily on your shoulders. So finding and holding onto the right mindset is vital to the future of your company, regardless of your goals.

How many times have you told someone that they "can't do that" or said, "That won't work"? Every time you say that to someone else, someone's saying it to you! Worse still is when you say those phrases to yourself: *I can't, it won't, I don't.* They kill your ambition. Self-doubt, that little devil sitting on your shoulder uttering those *can't* words to you, can be destructive. Here's how one of my clients fought, and won the battle with his doubts.

54

Peter had a solid business supplying air-conditioning units to business customers. He was very good at what he did, but he always had doubts. Did clients really value him? Would they pay? He was petrified of losing a client, of screwing up, of a project not working. He was a glass half-empty rather than a glass half-full person. So what changed?

Working together, we built a real, not perceived, view of the business and concentrated on the positive stuff. We talked about the business to existing clients, prospects, and suppliers, in fact to anyone we could. We changed the way he thought: instead of "I can't," the words became "How can I...?" Banishing the words "I can't" was hard, but the more Peter used the "How can I...?" question, the more his confidence improved. Positivity grew, smiles returned, prices increased, and new customers were secured.

Peter hasn't looked back since. He still has doubts, but he recognises them and works hard to uncover the positive thoughts. The business has grown beyond his expectations and he realises that life is much better when you look at the positive side.

We all feel energised by the positive, energetic people we meet; they give us a boost. Surround yourself with positive people and build your team with people who have positive attributes. Don't be the downbeat, depressing, moaning, whining bore; it's a surefire way to drive clients away. If you are surrounded by those kinds of people – jettison them now!

- What did you tell yourself today that you couldn't do or wouldn't work? Instead of focusing on the downside, change the question to "How can I do..." or "How can I make this work?"

- Try to stop the "You can't" comments when you talk to your team. Ask them "How can you..." questions instead. Likewise, get them to ask you "How can I...?" questions rather than making "I can't" comments.

- Practise what you preach. Avoid telling anyone that they can't, especially the kids!

Do you really want to?

If, like the majority of business owners, you started your business because you loved doing the work or because you have a specific technical expertise that you could sell, then you now have a decision to make. Do you want a company that you work *in* or a growing business that you *run*?

Running a business which allows you to do the work you love is great. Our country is so much better for lifestyle businesses: happy business owners earning enough to live on, doing what they love, and contributing to the economy and their community. I for one celebrate those people. But if you want more than that, then you can have it – at a price.

"I'm going to double my business in three years" trips off the tongue easily, but what does that mean for you personally, for your people, and for the operations of your business? Are you prepared to…

- learn new skills (some will be tough to master)?
- commit to the extra effort and extra hours that are needed in the early years?
- challenge yourself to build a better business and seek out new opportunities?
- try something new, radical, or different?
- shift your work focus so that you are working *on* the business, not *in* it?
- stick with it when the going gets tough?
- lead your team and empower them to deliver your vision of the future?

It's as easy to just say "Yes" to all of those questions, without thinking it through quickly. The journey will be tough as well as rewarding, so ask yourself whether or not you really want to – and be true to yourself.

Paul set up The Engineering Co Ltd 20 years ago. He was a brilliant precision engineer; he loved designing and making bespoke parts that solved his client's problems. He had a great client list, with high-profile names as well as a good spread of companies that he supplied. He spent every minute he could on the shop floor. He always found important things to do in the factory, because that was where he wanted to be. But the company was heading in the wrong direction.

It was tough: cash flow was tight, paperwork was ignored, customers drifted away and metal stock was everywhere but never where or when it was needed! It was chaos and soon his six engineers would have to find themselves another job. As the business owner, Paul should have been running the business, but instead he was working in the business, on the machines. What he really wanted to do was to solve clients' engineering challenges. He wanted to make things, not to run a business.

Paul's passion and enthusiasm for his craft had rubbed off on his daughter, Emma. She gained an engineering degree and worked for BAE Aerospace for a couple of years. The difference between them was that Emma really wanted to run a successful company – to turn her father's business into the success it should be. Emma understood engineering, but recognised that her father's love of the hands-on would always mean that the business suffered. She wanted to change that and so did Paul.

The solution? Emma came into the business as managing director, to run it. Paul became chairman and technical director, because he loved the work so much. This allowed him to concentrate 100% on delivering brilliant solutions for their clients without having to stress about the money, paperwork, or red tape.

Emma, safe in the knowledge that her dad was an exceptional technician, concentrated on stabilising and building strong foundations for the business, before they could start to grow up. The transition was tough for a little while but what a transformation in the company! Sales were soon on the up, new customers were won, lost customers returned, cash flow and profit got back on track, and the right metal stock was in the right place. Two very happy, fulfilled people and one successful business.

⮕ Time for a bit of soul-searching. Look back at the questions above. I know that you may want to say "Yes" to all of them, but take some time to think through the implications. As you jump into your car tonight or have your shower in the morning, ask yourself "How can I prepare myself for this journey?"

⮕ While we've focused on positivity in this section, I want you to have a look at your fears – all those nagging doubts. Let's get them out on the table and deal with them now. Better to know what you're facing, so you can prepare. I'm grateful to *The Artist's Way* for the inspiration for the next exercise. Take a sheet of paper and draw four columns.

1 In column one, write your *negative thoughts.*
2 In column two, next to each negative, write down what it *costs* you to have that negative thought. For example, the cost of thinking "I can't write a book" means you never will.
3 In column three, write down the *benefit* of each negative thought. For example, "I'm the best unpublished author ever!" or "I won't have to deal with rejections or spend time writing!"
4 Finally, in the last column, write *the exact opposite* to what you wrote in column one. For example, "I will write a book and publish it." As you are reading this book, you'll know that I overcame my doubts!

Take the time you need

Do you turn up for work every day because you feel that you ought to? Are you the first person there in the morning, the last one to go at night, and the only one in at the weekend? Do you feel that you *should* be at your desk all the time because you're the boss? Or do you *have* to be there to make sure everything happens as it should do?

Stop. You *are* the boss, you *do* have a choice. In fact, you owe it to the business to take some time out. If you're working in the business all day every day, when will you get time to think, plan, seek out and explore opportunities, or just to clear your head of stuff? Taking time out or making time for important things is, well, important. Unfortunately, many business owners assume that being at work all the time is good leadership. So let's see the benefits of giving yourself permission to take a break and clear your head.

There are three types of important time, in addition to your productive time: thinking time, planning time, and clear-head time. Thinking time happens best when you just let your mind wander. No interruptions and a change of scene help. Planning time is time to work hard on a specific problem. Clear-head time happens when you don't think about work, to refresh your mind, such as weekends, holidays, or the odd half-day out of the office for something completely different. (For me, it's golf.)

There are many reasons why you need to give yourself permission to be away from the company. While the day-to-day running of the company is important, so is your time away from routine work.

Planning time

- Reflect on what happened, what didn't, and what can be improved. How did your actual performance match up to the budget? Sort through all of the facts, get a clearer perspective.
- Make adjustments to get you back on track or to set a new course. Reforecast the forthcoming months.
- Identify problem areas; study problems from different angles.
- Seek out opportunities.
- Clarify your goals.
- Assess whether it's time to change direction.

It's easy to be consumed with the day-to-day tasks of running a business. All too often, planning time is overtaken by the in-tray, emails, phone calls, and client and staff demands. You have to make your planning time sacrosanct.

I have several clients who have a Monday morning or Friday afternoon status meeting, where they reflect on what has or hasn't happened and plan the immediate next steps.

Every week is great; at minimum, every month you should review and plan. The perfect time is when the monthly management accounts and profit-and-loss statements are prepared for the previous month. How often do you just flick through the accounts and put them to one side when you should be taking time to really understand them? If there is one meeting that should never be cancelled it's your monthly senior management meeting (or board meeting). It's far too important to cancel and even a day's delay could have a negative impact. But make it effective planning time, where the outcomes are action-orientated.

Each quarter, you should set aside more time to review the entire business, its performance and any opportunities and threats on the horizon. Then replan, reforecast and rebudget.

➲ Take one planning item from your to-do list – perhaps an upcoming exhibition or the next quarter's marketing strategy – and book an afternoon out of the office. Go somewhere else and work on planning, nothing else. This is your planning time.

Thinking time

- Carve out quiet time to think, with no interruptions.
- Explore what's going on around you. What are your competitors up to, what new demands might your customers or clients have, what are your suppliers planning next?
- Explore creative options: ask yourself the "What if…?" question.
- Experience something different.
- Re-engage with your dream.

When there is so much going on, so much to do, so many plates spinning or wobbling, you don't have chance to think about anything. But if you are to have any chance at all of moving your business forward, you must have time to think: quiet time, time to mull, time to ask the "What if…?" questions. *Too busy to think* is a poor excuse and you have to find productive thinking time.

You don't need loads of thinking time, but you need good thinking time. Several short bursts, a couple of hours here and there, will be enough. Take yourself away from the day-to-day business environment, remove distractions, and find a place where you can think.

My writing coach, Megan Kerr, taught me a great little exercise. Set 10-15 minutes aside to work on just one issue. Work hard at it for that short time period. Just as you finish, ask yourself a positive question, such as "How can I improve…?", "What options do I have?, "How can I get *x* to work?", "What is the real problem?" and so on. Now go away and do something completely different. One of the things Megan suggested was doing the housework, which is never much fun for me, although it proved to be very productive! Why? Because when you go and do something completely different, you can let your subconscious go to work on the last tricky problem that you gave it to think about.

You have to be disciplined and organised. Start these new disciplines now and very soon you'll wonder how you managed to function without any thinking time.

⮑ Try asking yourself one question – a "How can I…?" question. Now go and do something different: go for a swim, take a walk, do anything but work. Don't rush the answer; let your subconscious solve it for you. It may take you an hour or three, or a day or two, but the answer will come.

Clear-head time

- Spend time deliberately *not* thinking about work – or anything much, for that matter.
- Recharge your batteries – you can't run effectively on empty.
- Allow your subconscious to go to work on some of those knotty problems.

Holidays are critical. You need time to unwind and clear your head of the day-to-day clutter. Remind yourself what a good night's sleep is all about and the importance of family, reconnect with the important people in your life and have some "me" time. Holidays need to be long enough to make a difference: you're not indispensable.

Every week, in fact every day, you need clear-head time. Weekends are so easily consumed with work, but not giving yourself a break means that you won't be refreshed and raring to go on Monday morning. We can't holiday every week, but we can find time to do something completely different, so that our work brain gets a rest. As the saying goes, "A change is as good as a rest."

Remember the ash cloud of 2010, when flights were cancelled for days and weeks? Many business owners were trapped thousands of miles from home and work. But businesses carried on without them. In fact, many would have thrived without the boss. Staff love the opportunity to step up and take responsibility while the boss is away. Don't feel guilty.

If you have never let your team make a decision without your confirmation before, then they never will be able to do so. In my early corporate life, I travelled a lot, usually in the car. My team must have had a sixth sense because as soon as I jumped into the car, the car phone always rang – one of my team needing to ask a question or wanting some help. Of course, I answered their queries and moved on to the next call to solve that problem too.

My epiphany came because I left my phone behind one day. I was so stressed about the office I stopped at a phone box; I'd been out of contact for most of the day and I thought it was probably chaos back at base. It wasn't. My team was fine and because they couldn't get hold of me, they made decisions and choices. All was good and they were proud that they had just got on with it – and so was I! That was probably one of the best business lessons I learnt early in my career: to set the team objectives and then let the team deliver, with me exerting a light touch rather than a heavy hand. From that day forward I was less available to the team, to its benefit. You need clear-head time and your staff will do fine without you.

Finding clear-head time can, on the face of it, be a challenge, but in reality it's easy. Your day can incorporate it naturally. On the drive to and from work, turn off your phone and the radio, and think. In the shower or the bath, don't plan and ponder: let your mind float. If life is really chaotic, get up fifteen minutes before everyone else, make a brew, and sit and think – don't even consider turning the radio on. Walk the dog – or just walk. Walking is very rhythmic and you find that your thoughts relax and tumble about much more easily as the walking rhythm builds.

➲ Just get away from it all – clear the clutter that is clouding your mind – book a holiday, now! Don't stop there; block out two more holidays. Try not to leave more than three months between them.

I'm too busy to...

This is the phrase I hear most when I start working with a new client: "I'm too busy to..."

I ask, "Busy achieving what?"

We can all be busy doing nothing and I admit that I have paper-shuffling and I'll-just-tidy-up days too. But isn't it amazing how productive you can be when you have a massive deadline looming? The faster the clock ticks, the faster your fingers move over the keyboard! When you're growing a business, you can't use the "I'm too busy" excuse. You need to *find* time to do the important things, so let's see how.

I could say "Get up earlier!" or "Work harder to clear your in-tray!" but that's not going to help much – not for long anyway. It's not about how hard you work; it's about what you work on. You can easily become a busy fool and that's an expensive option! In my experience, many business owners and managers are doing just that. No matter how busy you are, ask yourself, "Busy achieving what?"

Your business must always be about achievements. At school, we focus on achieving a good grade, on passing exams, on getting a certificate, or on hearing, "Well done." But why, when we get into the business world, do we stop focusing on achieving and instead just start doing?

Knowing what you want to achieve has to be the starting point. Set your achievements or goals and work steadily towards them. Each achievement will have a series of mini-achievements or milestones: achieve each one and you'll have achieved your goal.

If you miss deadlines or never seem to get that new product launched, then sit back, take a deep breath, and review what you need to achieve. Then give that 100% of your attention.

You need to work smarter, but how? When you work for eight hours a day, you'll be doing lots of things that you don't need to do. Some might need to be done, but not by you – you're too expensive! Some, you can just stop doing – the things that don't take you nearer your goal. Take a critical look at what you are doing every day. Set out three columns and head **delegate**, **terminate**, and **automate**. Next, allocate every single task you do to one of the headings.

- **The Terminate list** is a no-brainer – just terminate these tasks – don't do them anymore. Time saved.

- **The Delegate list** should be relatively easy. For example, if you're a solopreneur, a virtual assistant is a great resource – use (and pay) only when you need them. If you have a team of people working for you, then get them to free up some time by doing this same exercise, so you can delegate to them with a clear conscience.
- **For the Automate list,** you need to look (and probably learn) where technology can solve your problems and save you time. Ask others around you how technology can help you work smarter and achieve more.

I believe that every business owner should be drawing at least £100,000 of personal income from their business. Of course, this does mean you have to put more than £100,000 worth of value back into the business. You can't do that if you're sweating the small stuff or doing work that someone else can do better, more quickly, and more cheaply. £59 is the magic number. Here's how:

£100,000 divided by 42 weeks (time off for holidays, training, etc) = £2,380 per week

Assuming a 40-hour week, £2,380 divided by 40 = £59.52 per hour

If you can delegate or outsource a task for less than £59 per hour, you're saving the business money. Now you have the time to achieve the important stuff that only you can do.

Sam and Bob had been running their IT Company for seven years and had fallen into the "I'm too busy" trap. Neither of them was drawing £100,000 and they were working 70+ hours a week. If they weren't careful, they soon would be working for the minimum wage! Sam did all the bookkeeping. This was a nightmare task for him, but he thought it was important enough for him to carry on doing it. Credit control had no control, cash flow was in a bad way, and costs were running out of control. Clients just waited to be chased before they paid their invoices.

It took Sam a whole day, once a week, just to keep on top of the paperwork and try to exercise some control. Monthly management accounts and key performance indicators (KPI) eluded him. Eight hours at £59 an hour is £472. Now add at least three more days for Sam to prepare the quarterly VAT return: another £1,400.

He made one change in the business: he hired a bookkeeper for one day a week, which cost the company £240. That was an immediate saving of £232, plus Sam now had a completely free day to work on building the business.

Within four weeks, the bank balance was the highest it had ever been. The bookkeeper not only had the accounts in good order but had collected all the outstanding monies. Mandatory wage reporting (RTI) was up to date, monthly management accounts were produced, and work had started on a set of KPIs.

Now Sam and Bob know exactly where the business is and isn't performing. They know what money is outstanding, and what they owe and when – no more stress worrying if the accounts and regulatory reporting are accurate and in good order. Sam has time to launch a new revenue stream into the business, something that had been on the back burner for quite a while.

Sam didn't like doing the books: he didn't really understand it and he made mistakes, which the bookkeeper found. He engaged an expert who knew what they were doing and could do it more quickly and accurately than he could. The moral of the story is, if it costs you less to outsource, then do it.

➲ Write down everything you did last week in 15-minute slots. Now find yourself some coloured pens.

➲ Pick up the red pen and cross out what you can terminate.

➲ Take a blue pen and underline what you can delegate, either to an employee or outsourcing. Consider…

1 setting up meetings
2 social media
3 bookkeeping, VAT, payroll and tax returns, invoicing, expenses
4 warehousing, despatch, and deliveries
5 event and exhibition planning, logistics, and bookings
6 research
7 stationery and office supply orders
8 copywriting, PowerPoint presentations, proofreading, speech writing, blogging, podcasts, etc
9 emails, in and out

⤵ Take a green pen and highlight the tasks that you should be able to automate.

This exercise should remove at least 50% from your to-do list. If not, do it again until you've removed 50%. Now take that new free time to build your growing business.

If you struggle to focus on the important things or to actually get anything done, try some of these tips, which I've collected throughout my working life. There is usually at least one that can help you: it's just a case of finding the combination that works for you.

- **Write three tasks** down the night before and leave it on your desk. When you arrive the next day, you can be at full throttle within minutes of starting work.
- **Complete three tasks** within your first hour of work.
- **Discover the times of the day when you are super-productive** and schedule important work to be done then.
- **Try the 18-minute rule:** set the timer on your phone to go off in 18 minutes. Take one task and work only on that. You'll either finish within 18 minutes or you'll be on such a roll you'll only need a few more minutes to complete the task. There are 26 18-minute chunks in a working day – that's 26 tasks. Before, it took me half a day to write a blog post, but now it's 18 minutes and a small fee to my VA to post it, do the SEO, and tweet it. Suddenly I'd found another 222 minutes – or twelve more 18-minute chunks – to work on the business. My husband jokes that the 18-minute alarm gets more attention than he does!

- **Focus on achieving rather than doing.** Before you start each task, quickly ask yourself if you should be doing this or if there's someone better, quicker, or cheaper who can do it. Be clear about what you're going to achieve when you do a task. If it doesn't move the business forward, someone else should be doing it.
- **Turn off your phone and your email** for an hour, close the door, and get to it. Tell your team that you are not to be disturbed unless the building is burning down!
- **Leave the office for two hours** twice a week during office hours and go somewhere else to work. Take just one task with you and focus only on that task. If you can, try to use one of the two-hour sessions as thinking time.
- **Finish it, all of it.** One trap we all fall into is not finishing anything before we start something new. When you go back to complete a task, you have to get yourself back up to speed and that wastes time.
- **Focus on the important.** It might be urgent, but if it's not important, it shouldn't be done first. If it's urgent *and* important, do it now!
- **Terminate, delegate and automate.** Reduce your list every week until you're only doing the important stuff.

Reignite your dream

Remember the days before you started your business? The energy, drive, passion, and determination that drove you to launch the company? You'd celebrate small successes, burn the midnight oil on new projects, go back to the drawing board when things went wrong; you were invincible. Is it still like that? Are you still celebrating, burning the midnight oil, reworking things and making improvements; are you still invincible?

No? Then you need to reignite your dream or build a new dream. In this section, we'll discover how important your dreams are and consider the negative impact when you lose sight of your dream.

The euphoria of a new venture gives us a burst of energy, an overwhelming need or desire to succeed, a bit like a shot of adrenaline. We hope that the reality matches the dream, but that doesn't always happen first time. It's too easy to fall into the trap of working in the business rather than on your dream. It creeps up on you and then suddenly, there you are, worn out and tired.

Most of us work to live rather than living to work. Some people are workaholics; they tend to be the "work hard, play hard" types. I remember feeling dismayed when a colleague said that she lived for work. She was so obsessed with her work that she had few, if any, friends. When she went on holiday, she went alone. I imagined her lying on a sunbed in a beautiful place, still working for her boss.

Life is too short to live for work; we really must choose to work to live. As a business owner, you're privileged to have more freedom to choose than if you were working for someone else. You have the opportunity to realise your dream and shape your personal and business future.

If your business life is not okay, then your personal life is going to suffer too. Make sure you get a good balance between your personal and business goals. If the business hasn't turned out to be what you dreamt it would be, you have got to turn it around and quickly. With a business life full of drudgery, you lose your spark, your mojo, your passion. Now is the time to stop and get it back. Pulling yourself out of the rut isn't easy, though: you might need some time to think and replan, perhaps someone to help you rediscover why you started the business in the first place, reignite your dream, even build a new one.

Sean ran a successful investment brokerage with his partner, but his business partner really didn't want to be there. The atmosphere was depressing; everybody was miserable; the business was just limping along. Sean didn't want to be there either – any excuse to leave early or come in late, and he took it. Doing the work was so disheartening that he started to think about throwing in the towel, but he didn't.

His wife was a passionate gardener and had started selling plants and cut flowers at the local market. Easter and Mother's Day were approaching and she knew it would be busy, so she enlisted Sean's help at the weekend to sell the cut flowers for her while she concentrated on the plants. Sean loved it, chatting to customers and encouraging people to buy flowers even if that wasn't on their shopping list. He was buzzing at the end of the day, with a big smile on his face and eyes sparkling, something that had been missing for a while.

Reflecting on his Saturday job, Sean realised that he loved being with clients, selling and helping them. He wanted and needed to change the way his own business was running. He could do it. He reignited his passion for his own company by doing something completely different.

For the next few Saturdays, Sean was selling flowers. He loved the smiles he put on people's faces, especially when they told him how much they had enjoyed their flowers all week and so would buy some more. He soon realised that he loved being with clients, selling and helping them, and that was missing in his own business. He wanted and needed to change the way his own business was running. He couldn't continue like this.

He planned to inject the passion back into the business and the first task was to talk to his partner. His partner couldn't get excited about the business anymore and decided that he wanted to sell his shares. Sean snapped them up and set about building a bigger, better, more Grown-Up business – all because by doing something different, he'd reignited his passion, vision, and dream for the business.

Losing your mojo tends to creep up on you gradually. One bad day, followed by another, and soon your dream is in tatters. It might be that the dream you had was never going to translate into reality. If that's the case, now is the time to pause, reflect, and change your dream.

- ➲ I want you to dream, but not about your business. First I want you to paint a picture of your personal dream. Think about family, friends, holidays, homes, cars, interests, and goals. Perhaps you only want to work three days or five mornings a week, or to sell the business and retire.

- ➲ Now that you have your personal dream clear in your mind, you can concentrate on developing your business dream. Here are some questions for you:

1 How much do you *have to* earn versus what you *want to* earn?
2 When do you want to retire, reduce your hours, or go part-time?
3 Are you planning to sell the business or pass it on to the next generation? When will that be?
4 How much time do you want to spend at work and how much on your own interests?
5 What do you need to put in place in your company, so that you can...
   i) have the income you want?
   ii) have the time off that you crave?

You've cleared the obstacles and strengthened the first few rungs on the business ladder. Your dream is painted: you can now hold onto it even during those dark days. You've given yourself time out of the business for your thinking and planning time and you have some tactics to help you be ultra-productive. Your goals are set. You're growing up from the Early Years stage to become a Teenager.

Chapter 4

Time to Get Some Help

If running a successful, sustainable business were easy, everyone would be doing it. The reality is that more people than ever are starting their own business, but many haven't thought it through. It's so simple to go online and set up a company – so simple that too many do it on their own and get it wrong. They don't get any help before they start and even less when they're up and running, believing that because they run a business, they should know how to do it!

I know that managing a business is lonely. You're isolated, with no one to share your fears and concerns with or to help you sort out a problem. Most of my clients have supportive partners at home, but they just don't want to take their work home to them.

99.9% of business owners need help and now is the perfect time to get your support in place. Whether that's staff, advisors, outsourcers, experts, a sounding board, or a shoulder to cry on, you're going to need help. You won't be able to do it on your own. Where would Lord Sugar be without Margaret and Nick? When people ask me about my work I often say, "I'm the boss's boss," so that's where we'll start.

Who's your boss?

Like most business owners, you've probably worked for someone else. You had a boss, someone who told you what to do and how to do it. You could ask them for help. They would keep you on track with deadlines and make sure that you delivered on time and within your budget. You could go home and forget about work until the next day. You're the boss now and you don't have a boss anymore. The question is do you need one? Let's see.

I bet you've sat in your office and said, "I'll finish that report by the end of the week" or "I'll make an appointment with x client" but didn't do it. On Monday morning, you say the same thing; again, it doesn't happen. You tell yourself you're so busy you don't have time, but you'll do it next week. Suddenly a month or two has passed, figures are down, and it's only now you start kicking yourself because you didn't do what you said you would. A whole month's delay: you've lost time, you've lost opportunities, and you've certainly lost money.

The reality is that there's no one to enforce your deadline; no one is going to tell you off or make you squirm. The only person who gets their stuff on time is the tax man: you can't afford to make him angry, can you? So who do you report to, apart from the tax man? As the business grows, you'll soon be planning with and reporting to a board or your shareholders. They certainly won't be happy if you miss your deadlines.

Let's take another scenario. You have a great idea and you're so motivated that you get everything in place and launched in record time. Wow, super-productive! Soon you discover it was a really bad idea. You start asking yourself why you didn't see the obvious problems, why you didn't stop and think about what you were doing or whether you could have done it differently. Once again you've lost time, lost out on better opportunities, and probably lost lots of money.

If you don't have a boss and you can see yourself in the examples above, then it's time to get one. But who do you choose?

- a mentor: they'll help guide you to become accountable
- a business partner: joint directors are able to hold each other responsible
- a business coach: I'm the boss to many of my coaching clients at some point
- a non-executive director or a formal board
- an advisory board, if you don't have a formal board
- investors or shareholders: they'll be looking for their return, so they'll make sure you stay on track

If you want someone who's been there, done it, and got the T-shirt, then you need a mentor who'll guide you through the maze. A business coach will keep you on track, tease out your own goals, identify and overcome problems with you. A formal board of directors will be there to help direct the business, to ensure everything is legal and correctly run. Non-executive directors bring an external perspective, expertise, experience, and a precious black book! An advisory board advises you, but doesn't direct you. They meet with you regularly to assess progress, adjust plans, reforecast, and help to knock down any barriers that your business encounters. Advisory boards are commonplace in the tech start-up arena.

I recently worked with some Pfizer employees who were being made redundant when the Sandwich plant closed down. I helped them to work through their own start-up business plans. Of the 20 or so groups I worked with, 12 didn't launch. They all had great plans and the technical expertise to deliver them, but were they really going to be able to run a business? Throughout our discussions and planning sessions, it became clear that many of them realised that they needed a boss who would tell them what to do and when.

Faced with the reality of running their own company, they realised that the discipline, focus, and lack of time to work as a technician were not for them. They were all highly qualified, intelligent experts who managed teams within a clear structure, but they relished the large corporate culture. Swapping that structure, order, and direction to become a business owner was a dream that quickly fizzled out.

Megan was my boss when it came to writing this book. Her directions: 4,000 words a week, rewrite this section, restructure that section, edit it, cut 10% of waffle words, find a publisher, do a pitch and sell the book! Only once did I miss a deadline – slap on the wrist for me, but I didn't do it again. I didn't want to let her down. I wanted to get the book finished for myself, obviously, but I needed someone to be my boss!

Don't just find any old boss: you've got to work with them, not against them. Find someone who has the right skills and values, someone you can get to know, like, trust, and respect.

- ⮑ Talk to other business owners. Who do they have as their boss? Do they have coaches, mentors, or advisors that they could introduce to you?
- ⮑ Decide if you want someone who knows you and your faults or an outsider, who is not going to let you get away with anything.
- ⮑ Pull all of your thoughts together into a checklist before you start to approach prospective bosses, to make sure that you find the right person.
- ⮑ Sit down and make a list of everyone you know who might fit the role. Now cross out the ones that don't feel right. For those that remain, take a little more time to think if they're the right person for you.

Accountable people and expert panels

It's hard to have a debate or argument with yourself. Trying to play the devil's advocate doesn't work either. How do you ask yourself the questions you don't even know that you need to ask? It's tough on your own and if you don't have a boss, a board, or shareholders, who do you get to help you with those debates, questions and challenges? You need an accountable person and a panel of experts.

Accountable person

An accountable person is a bit like a boss. They're able to hold you to account, to test and challenge you. They become your sounding board, tutor, and mentor, a shoulder to cry on, a pat-on-the-back person to encourage you or the custodian of the child reins to hold you back. As we established in the last section, you should have a boss, but there's no reason why you shouldn't have an accountable person or two in your team too.

Your bank manager, accountant, and lawyer could be accountable people for you, but many don't have the time or the skills to work with you. Do include them as members of your panel of experts though.

Panel of experts

A panel of experts is a great way for you to access technical expertise when you can't afford or don't need their services full time. Your panel of experts will always be there for you, holding you to account for delivering your side of the work: just give them permission. They're there for you to call on them for help.

In addition to your bank manager, accountant, and lawyer, other expert panel members would include your PR, web, and marketing agency, your suppliers, a selection of your customers, IT support, and so on. There is such a wide range of people who could help – but don't ask everyone you know to join your expert panel!

Finding an accountable person and constructing your panel of experts is as important as recruiting any senior manager or a non-executive director. Skills are important, but it's critical that their style and attitude suits you. Start by working out what your main problems are.

- Do you lack skills, expertise, or experience in certain areas?
- Do you need a sounding board, someone to bounce ideas around and test out your theories?
- Do you need a different perspective or expertise from another industry?
- Are you missing expertise in your field? Do you want a big hitter, someone who's well-known and can open doors in your industry?

- Do you miss deadlines, lose focus, find it hard to concentrate, keep getting pulled back into the day-to-day? Are you the one helping to pack the orders?
- Do you need someone to help shape your dreams, understand the risks, and share your fears, problems, and successes with?
- Do you need an opposite to you – a methodical systems person or perhaps a creative to complement you?
- Do you lack confidence?

Above all your accountable person must be non-judgemental and capable of adding value, correcting you, and helping you to improve. Accountable people aren't permanent: they change as the demands of the business change.

Debbie had run a successful business for many years. It was profitable but stuck and unable to grow. She didn't know what to do next; she was risk-averse and her confidence was low.

A chance meeting with one of my colleagues, Phil, turned her world around. He built her confidence and helped her to plan and understand what risks she was prepared to take. He opened her eyes to a different dream. He chastised her when she went off track and didn't do what she said she would. He kept her to deadlines that he'd made her set. She had found her accountable person.

The business started to grow, as did her confidence. Suddenly she was on her way: new premises, new revenue streams (planned ages ago but never implemented), new staff to help (she just hadn't got round to employing those extra people last year), new customers, and new systems put in place.

Debbie is brilliant technically, but desperately needed someone to hold her accountable so that she actually worked on the business and not in it. She doesn't regret any of the changes since she found Phil as her accountable person. She just wonders why it took her so long – but then she knows the answer to that too!

Time for a glass of wine or a cuppa, and pen and paper (or in Debbie's case, a laptop):

- ➲ Make a list of all of your shortcomings, the problems and challenges the business has today, and gaps you've found. What do you need help with? Review the questions earlier in the section to help your thought process.
- ➲ Put the list in priority order, with the most important aspect for you at the top. For example, if you really need a sounding board to test out plans, ideas, and tactics, rather than someone to make you do something, a sounding board is first on the list.
- ➲ Who do you have in your expert panel? What gaps do you need to fill?
- ➲ Now you have your checklist for your accountable person. Review this list alongside the one you developed for your boss. If there are lots of similarities, then you should consider having your boss as your accountable person too.

Everyone needs some support

However focused, driven, organised, and knowledgeable you are, everyone needs a bit of moral support now and then. Sometimes it's knowing that your partner or mum is proud of you or hearing someone say "Thank you" or "Well done." Who do you turn to when you need a bit of a boost, when you've had the day from hell, when you're tired, ill, sad, depressed, lonely, lost, or confused?

As the boss, you probably don't feel able to confide in your employees when you're feeling down, but you do need someone to help you regain your oomph. Let's explore how to build a support network.

Your first support network was your parents, then you added friends, teachers, more friends, sports coaches, piano teachers, ballet teachers, or the scout leader. Grandparents, aunts and uncles provided additional support as well. You had different people for different types of support: parents for well-being and financial support; friends to help you when a boyfriend dumped you, when spots broke out, or to borrow a frock; your teachers, coaches, and guides to support your learning and help you gain more skills. As you embark on your growing-up journey, you'll need a support network as well as your boss or accountable person.

The golden rule is that the people you choose to be in your support network need to be givers, not takers. We've all come across both types. You need people who give without asking and do it willingly. There will be times along the way when you can give back to them willingly, but your task here is to find the givers first. I'm sure that you're already giving as part of someone else's support network.

Family, partners, and friends might be at the top of your list, but they may not be the best ones to have. Whatever we do, they love us, always telling us we're the best. They find it hard to find fault, but sometimes that's what we need most. Rose-coloured spectacles won't help. Likewise, close friends might not criticise you. Certainly you'll benefit from good friends who can administer a great night out when you need it – but that's not quite the same as a support network.

You need to hear the reality from your support network, even if you don't want to. Learning to hear the tough messages is important. It's no use being told something's a great idea when it's clearly not. Your support network must be bold and confident enough to point that out. When you're choosing your support network, ask, "Does this person tell me when I'm wrong?"

Another good test is to ask yourself whether you can confide in them. There will be delicate or sensitive information to share, so find people you can trust to keep your information secret as well as help you work through your challenges. Perhaps an experienced business person can help?

Small-business peer-to-peer groups are great support networks. It can be quite hard to join one as an outsider, so the best solution is to build your own group. You want five or six people who meet and build a safe environment in which to share. It's unlikely that your weekly or monthly paid-for business club will be able to give you this quality of support.

During my corporate life I had the pleasure of being mentored by a FTSE Top10 Deputy CEO. He taught me so much and building a strong support network was one of the best lessons. We'll call him Matthew. He shared this with me when I was wrestling with a tricky issue.

He was part of a peer-to-peer group and had been for the past 20 years, with the same seven people: no one left or joined in all those years. They met up once a quarter for dinner, but in between meetings, everyone was available to each other as a sounding board, for technical advice, or just for a few words of wisdom. There was complete trust in the group and many a tricky problem was solved with help from the support network. Matthew was a great leader, businessman, and person; many of his skills and traits were enhanced by his peer-to-peer group. Inspired by him, I started my own peer-to-peer group some years ago; all of us would agree it's a great support network.

⊃ Build your own peer-to-peer group of like-minded people: five or six others who can meet up about once every couple of months.
⊃ Join a new group-coaching group – one that runs for a fixed period with no visitors. Complete the facilitated group coaching and if suitable it can then pivot into a peer-to-peer group.

Who do you know who can help?

We've looked at people who can help you to be effective, focused, and supported, but there's another group of people that you need to engage with: your industry. These are your networks. You'll have several already and within these networks you'll be able to find the real gems who can help you. Many of us shudder when we hear "networking" mentioned. There are even workshops on how to network effectively! Suffice to say this is not a quick fix: it takes time to build your networks, engage with them, and reap rewards.

There are different types of networks to consider:

- your personal network
- business networks within your industry
- networking groups
- industry events and conferences
- peer-to-peer groups and their extended network
- online networks
- paid for networks

A network is a collection of like-minded people who're able to connect, discuss, and help each other; it's a forum to ask for help and to give it as well. For me, a network doesn't involve breakfast, that's not how I work best, though for many business owners they're a great forum. The success of groups such as BNI, 4N, and BOB is measured by their membership levels, longevity, and churn rates. Let's take a look at each type of network in turn.

1. Your personal network

This includes your extended family, friends from school and university, neighbours, interest groups, sports clubs, and so on. You know them all – some well, others not, but you do know them. At some point, we all ask our own personal network to help. A common question in our pub is "Do you know someone who can…?" We go to the people we know best for advice, help, or an introduction: can you help me move house, take me to this, show me how to do that, introduce me to this person, have a phone number for that person, et cetera.

Our personal network includes people we've selected rather than those forced upon us. (I guess the only exception to this is family members!) We naturally align ourselves with like-minded people – those with the same values, thoughts, and aspirations. Business failure rarely damages our personal network unless we've borrowed money from them and lost it! Over time our networks morph into something new. I have friends that I saw every week for years that I now see just a couple of times a year. Despite this, I can still ask them for help.

The shape of your network changes depending on what's happening to you at that time. As your needs change, you naturally look for people who can plug those gaps. In the end, our networks grow as we get older.

2. Networks in your industry

Most established industries have industry bodies, trade associations, committees, institutes, or federations. Their focus is to promote the industry and in some cases to regulate it. It is your choice to engage with them or not and decide how involved you become. These bodies offer a range of services: newsletters, conferences or exhibitions, forums, meetings, training, membership lists, lobbying, and always lots of experience and expertise within them. Membership fees and benefits vary, but it's always worth being connected to them.

A Grown-Up Business will seek to take an active role in any trade organisation. It will want to be at the forefront of any major or regulatory changes that might impact its business. It's also willing to share with others and generally help the industry improve standards.

When I worked in the concrete industry, members of the British Precast Concrete Federation and the lobbying group pulled together to present a case to the Highways Agency for concrete rather than metal barriers between motorway carriageways. They succeeded and as a result the whole industry benefited.

It's really worth getting to know your trade association: who are the influencers, the big hitters, the respected names? Make a point of getting onto their radar. You never know when you might need them.

3. Networking groups

In just about every town there are a number of different networking groups that hold events. These are not the subscription-based ones (more on those later); these are the pay-as-you-go ones, which are increasing in popularity.

They are usually established because of a common interest:

- a sector speciality: for example, creative, technology, or fashion
- a location
- a segment, e.g. women
- self-promotion
- education
- a problem to be solved, such as the closure of a major business locally
- golfing and sporting groups

My local landscape looks like this:

- creative and digital: at least three groups
- location: each main town has at least one group
- segment: Women in Business and Professionally Pink, to name a couple

- Muesli Mafia and Breakfast Friends are growing in several locations
- universities, enterprise hubs, chambers of commerce, Institute of Directors, FSB
- regional development areas also have location and specific industry groups
- as a golfer I've found several golf societies for business people!

I could attend a networking group every day of the week (sometimes two or three times a day) if I wanted to, but then I wouldn't get anything done!

Many say the principle of networking is to give, but I want to make sure that my time there is giving me value, too. Most have a speaker, so I always have the opportunity to learn something new, hear a different view, and meet new people. For me, networking isn't only about finding new clients: it's an opportunity to learn, to grow my network, and to have some intellectual conversation. I've learnt that each group has its own unwritten rules and type of person who attends. My suggestion is that you visit a few, try them out, and find the ones that work for you. You'll also meet the seasoned networker who pops up at just about every event you attend.

4. Industry events and conferences

Whether they are trade-specific or general events, this is another opportunity to learn and connect with new people. I use these opportunities to reconnect with people I know and touch base with my suppliers and clients outside of normal business constraints. Just turning up and seeing who you can spot is not the best use of your time and certainly not if you are exhibiting. You need a plan.

- Find out who's attending.
- List who you want to meet and connect with.
- Make appointments with key targets before you go – don't leave it to chance.
- Establish who can make introductions for you.
- Connect with people before you go and then again afterwards.

5. Peer-to-peer groups

In the last section we looked at peer-to-peer groups. These people are trusted, liked, and a strong network for you. Members know lots of people and will be happier to introduce you as a fellow peer-to-peer group member. As an extension of your peer-to-peer group you also have access to an extended network of very trusted contacts from the group. This is added reach and influence. LinkedIn has been great at showing us the sheer amount of reach we have – for example, at the time of writing, I have access to 7,782,226 connections. Now that's a network!

6. Online networks

20 years ago we didn't have to think about these, but today we ignore them at our peril. Not all social networks work for everyone. I use LinkedIn and Twitter daily, and Google+, Facebook, and Pinterest sporadically, but another business coach might have a different formula. The key to social networks is to be social. You have to engage with your selected audience, where they are, and that takes time. I don't have time to be equally social in every online network and the recipe above works for me; yours is bound to be different.

I've met some great people on Twitter and I've asked for help from followers as far afield as Australia. Pretty much everything is online these days – lots of free information, experts on forums, and interest groups all waiting for you to engage with them. But a quick health warning: networking online can take up a huge amount of time; be careful and use it wisely.

If you're already active online, then review what you do, how often, and what your objectives are. If you're new to social networking, join some networks and listen for a while to understand how they operate. If it's the right forum for you, join in; if not, find another. Online networking happens 24/7, every day of the year. My son uses social networks for his global business and there's always someone to help, even when he works through the night. He knows that like-minded people in his online network are awake and online somewhere in the world.

7. Paid-for networking

I've already said this is not for me, but for many business owners it's a fantastic forum and a great chance to get out and about, to see other business owners, and to get a different perspective.

The ones I have attended are very process-driven and demand that each member brings referrals to the meetings. This doesn't suit everyone: many dislike the pressure of finding referrals, especially in the early days when you haven't really got to know the other group members. They usually only have one person per trade, so competition is reduced, but this only works if the person holding the slot – the plumber, for example – is good at what they do and at responding to your referrals. As a result, some groups have a high turnover of members, whereas others are very stable. Be prepared to pay a joining fee and to sign up for at least a year, so choose wisely.

Networking is a necessary part of the Growing-Up Business journey. It will take different forms throughout the journey and will be different for different people. The key is not to focus on just one type of network: you'll need them all but in different measures at different times.

There are just as many ways to find someone who can help you as there are weeks in the year. We've all heard the saying, "It's not what you know, it's who you know." This next case study proves that who you know can be the difference between a huge success and a daily struggle.

Martin's young twin boys soon discovered that if they turned off the Sky box at the wall, the light went out – and on again when they switched the Sky box back on. Finally the Sky box gave up! So Martin set about designing a solution. He developed a great safety product to stop children (and adults!) from turning off a switch that shouldn't be turned off.

His design was fantastic, the patent secured, and the product materials chosen, prototyped, and tested. Everything was set: he knew his market, he knew the product inside out, and everyone he'd shown it to loved it. The product worked and people wanted it. But Martin didn't know where to start when it came to selling, especially to the major retailers. He was really stuck and couldn't do this on his own; he needed help.

I suggested that there must be someone he knew who could help. He did know an awful lot of people; but he couldn't think of anyone.

I encouraged him to take time to review his personal network: list everyone he knew and who they might know. He was a great mindmapper, so set about mapping everyone out. He called me a few days later to say that he had found the perfect person, and guess what? She lived two doors away and went horseriding with his wife every week. Sarah ran a successful company selling electrical beauty products to the major retailers and her partner ran the manufacturing plant in China. Problem solved.

⊃ Map your personal network. Mindmapping, like Martin did, is a great way, but lists work just as well. You'll need an hour's peace and quiet – perhaps use some of your planning time. Take a large sheet of paper (I usually use a flip chart) and put yourself in the middle. Plot everyone you know on the mind map or in a list. When you think you have everyone on the paper, review and see if there are more that you can add. Now take each person and run a strand, line or whatever mark you want to use to show how they are connected to other people you know. Try using different coloured pens to mark where connections link, where you need to find out more, or where they could be a useful connection because of who they know.

⊃ Review LinkedIn. Who are you connected to and who's missing? Make a list of the people you'd like to connect with, find them, and see how you're connected. You should be able to ask someone for an introduction.

⊃ Take time to review your social media activity or to learn more about it. There are lots of short workshops available locally.

⊃ Review networking opportunities in your area, try a few and see if they work for you, but don't commit to the subscription until you are sure.

⊃ Review what your trade association offers and how it could help you. Pick up the phone and have a chat with them.

How much does it cost?

My dad always said you get nought for nought in this world. If it's free, it's probably not worth it and if it seems too good to be true, it probably is.

Over the past decade, governments both national and local have offered free or subsidised schemes to help businesses to grow, export, innovate or raise finance. The landscape is changing and companies are now expected to pay. Of course, the private sector has always been paid for.

Whatever you do, you have to get the best help, expertise, and skills you can for a fair price. There is a financial price to pay and that might be easily done. The more challenging price is what you pay in terms of your commitment, extra work learning additional skills, improved focus, and planning. Working with any coach, consultant, advisor, or government scheme brings with it a lot of extra work; you'll need to be committed if you're going to benefit.

Time is the biggest cost, quickly followed by blood, sweat, and tears, then money, so be prepared. Many ex-business people (especially angel investors) are happy to help for free or just a small fee. Some call themselves mentors. In the UK, there's a mistaken idea that mentors are free of charge. That's not true, especially if you want the best person. Everyone should be paid for their expertise, just as you expect to be paid for a product or service that you sell.

As with all industries, there's a spread of fees. Non-executive directors command £500–£10,000 a day or £75,000–£200,000 a year. It's just the same as recruiting a member of staff: you'll be paying for their expertise and the value they can add to your company. Be fair.

Grown-Up Businesses will always pay for expertise, regardless of the hat that person wears. They'll also set out in writing what's to be achieved with that supplier. Start a great habit now and do the same. Begin with a list of achievables, find the right person to help, and pay them a fair rate. You'll need to engage with them for a while: they usually can't give their best contribution from just one or two interactions with you.

If you want free advice, look on the internet, but that probably won't give you the solution that you really need.

An accountant friend of mine went to see a potential client who had a very specific problem. The client was going to have to pay £35,000 unless the accountant could solve it for him. The accountant confirmed he could solve the problem and said that his fee was £10,000. The client agreed to pay the fee (spend £10,000 instead of £35,000, saving £25,000); the accountant solved the problem in an hour and submitted his fee. The client wasn't happy: £10,000 for an hour's work! That was the client's mistake. He wasn't paying for the accountant's time; he was paying for his expertise. Lacking that expertise would have cost the client £35,000.

➲ What is on your wish list: what absolutely has to be solved but you can't do it?
➲ Set out a mini project plan, specifying what has to be done by when and your budget.
➲ Use your networks to find a person who can help you solve that problem, agree the deliverables, and engage them to deliver the project for you.

Building the right team

As the business grows, you'll need to employ people to help you. You've spent lots of time and effort constructing your plans, defining your goals, setting your standards, and attracting customers, so when you employ people, they have to be the right people. As the business owner, you have a responsibility to build a dream team.

Having a great team working with and for you is the goal of every Grown-Up Business. Everyone faces the same way and strives towards the same goals, but has fun too. Recruitment can be difficult, but it's much easier if you plan and prepare before you start. There are six aspects you need to work on.

1 Your **organisation chart** – but don't fill it with people's names or job titles. Instead, construct it using tasks. Start with a complete list of everything that must be done in your organisation. Now plot those onto the organisation chart. You'll find natural groupings which will help you to define the job roles.

2 Write the **job description** using the organisation chart you've just completed.

3 From the job description, you can determine the knowledge and skills that you're seeking. To complete the **KASH model** (Knowledge, Attitude, Skills and Habits), you also need to consider the attitude and habits that you want to see in your potential employee.

4 Alongside the job description, you'll soon have your list of **work house-rules** (coming up in the next chapter). These are a clear statement about what it's like to work in your organisation.

5 You've already set your vision, goals, and objectives, and these will be part of your recruitment and selection process. This may be written in the form of a **brand manifesto** (also coming up in the next chapter).

6 Get some **help with a technical recruitment**, such as a finance manager.

With these tools in place, you now understand exactly what type of people you want to recruit into your dream team. Grown-Up Businesses take time over recruitment: rarely is it a single one-hour interview. Usually, it includes at least two interviews plus psychometric and practical tests, such as preparing and delivering a short presentation.

By investing time now to find the right person to slot seamlessly into your team, you'll avoid a lot of trouble later on. Remember the ABC Ltd sales director in chapter one? You don't want one of those.

The Blind Co had recently gone into liquidation. Peter and Paul bought the entire company, lock, stock and barrel, and set about rebuilding the company, the customer base, and their profits. Three months in, it didn't look good. They were really busy with new orders, but the figures weren't showing that. So what was going on? At one of our coaching sessions, Paul mentioned that the finance director was very defensive, criticising the bookkeeper and generally blaming everyone else. Alarm bells started to ring with me and we quickly arranged a further meeting to include the FD and a very business-focused accountancy specialist I knew. Peter and Paul understood the numbers, but they weren't accountancy-minded.

The meeting didn't go well. The FD was even more defensive, but also unable to answer some basic accountancy questions posed by the accounting specialist. It was becoming clear that the FD wasn't up to the job; in fact, his lack of skills and expertise was putting the company at risk again.

Peter and Paul took the important decision to remove the FD immediately and replaced her with an interim FD. Within hours, the new FD had identified fundamental errors and rectified them. Over the next few days, he uncovered and corrected even more problems. The existing bookkeeper, who was very good at her job, was also remotivated now that she had a boss who knew what was going on!

Once the accounts were straight, the interim FD was able to reduce his involvement to three days a month with the bookkeeper managing the daily transactions. The accounting system also now delivered a real-time dashboard so that Peter and Paul could make better decisions.

Peter and Paul didn't have enough accountancy expertise or the checks and balances in place to manage the FD they'd inherited, but when they uncovered a problem, they dealt with it swiftly. Today The Blind Co is running smoothly and Peter and Paul make much better decisions because they have confidence in the numbers and excellent advice from their part-time FD. They've also saved the salary of a full-time FD!

➲ Review the six-step process above and construct your organisation chart based on tasks, objectives, and deliverables. Try to ignore the people currently doing the role and focus on the jobs that need to be done.

➲ Sit back and compare your function-and-task organisation chart to your current chart. Do you need to make any changes? Does your team have gaps that you need to fill or duplications you need to remove?

Sometimes it's hard to accept that you can't do it all on your own. However much drive and passion you have or hours you work, you can't know it or do it all. Asking for help is not a weakness: it's a sign of strength. It shows that you're well on your way to becoming a Grown-Up Business.

Reflect on this chapter over the next week and start to review who helps you now and what extra help you need. Whatever help you need, don't delay – the sooner you get that help, the sooner you'll start to grow up.

Chapter 5

Set the Standards

Setting the right standards is a fundamental building block to becoming a Grown-Up Business. You have to set the rules, police them, refine them, and improve them while keeping your whole team focused on behaving, doing and saying the right things at the right time. It's the same as setting the boundaries of acceptability for a child: you make the rules, set the standards, lead by example, and reinforce the acceptable behaviour to get what you want.

If you don't have any standards, you need to find them quickly. A lot will already be hidden in the business; they just don't have a label saying "standards" or "rules". You'll be amazed at how many unwritten rules your business has developed over time – and how few you'll think are acceptable!

When you have a set of standards and rules, it removes the guesswork for your team. They don't have to spend time thinking whether they should or shouldn't; they just need to follow the rules!

In business, it's the ease with which we can ignore things that gets us into trouble. We're pressured for deadlines, we gloss over the problem or the work, we just don't do it, we let it drift. The result: deadlines slip, we miss opportunities, and we lose money. We get very frustrated and angry with ourselves when we don't get what we want, especially when it's our fault.

Now it's time to deal with those things which have been left on the back burner, untouched, and forgotten about – the things you've managed to do without, so far, but which will make a positive impact on your business. We'll look at standards and how to set them, develop your brand manifesto and work house-rules, and discover why problem solving and process development are critical skills and attitudes for every Grown-Up Business. It's time to leave the Teenager behind and grow into a Young Adult.

Setting your standards

In our own lives, we all have standards that we live by: being on time, having clean shoes, appropriate dress, sending thank-you notes after receiving presents, and so on. It comes as second nature. Likewise, we have our own values, our own version of acceptable behaviour, how we treat everyone we meet, what our families and friends mean to us, and how much we help our community too. These unwritten rules are the standards by which we each live our life – the tiller that keeps our own boat cutting a swathe through the water in the direction we want.

Your business is no different; it needs a set of standards that become the guiding beacon for everybody in your business to follow. It needs a set of standards and values which it applies day in, day out. Grown-Up Businesses don't settle for the minimally acceptable levels, either: they actively decide exactly what the standards are, they set those standards, and then they hit them every day.

As the business owner, you have the opportunity to dictate the standards that you set. They'll quite naturally develop from your own behavioural and social standards, and will follow the level of respect you have for the people that your business touches. They'll be dictated by your goals and your ambitions, too. Be clear about how your own standards and values affect and reflect your brand.

We'll see later in this chapter that your brand manifesto is your global statement of intent, your public declaration of purpose, your *raison d'être*. It will need some help coming to life. Writing it isn't enough – you have to define how it all works, then implement and maintain it. Setting the standards adds the detail and the how. Your work house-rules will help you drill down into the exact detail.

Setting your standards also goes hand in hand with making sure that the customer's experience is the same every time. A Grown-Up Business sets its standards and then consistently delivers them again and again, no exceptions ever. The standards you set to start with should be your desired, gold-level standards. If you only set the basic, minimum service-level, then everyone in your team will be happy to settle for the minimum they can get away with. It's hard to change behaviours upwards and people generally don't cope well with change, especially if they don't understand why the improvements are needed.

Service industries such as hairdressers, restaurants, and hotels are usually good examples of standard setting. In any town, there are several restaurants all trying to be different to each other and attract the right clientele with the standards they have set. Think about linen tablecloths and napkins, suited and booted waiting staff, leather bound menus (without spelling mistakes), and the expensive price tag. Contrast that with no tablecloth, paper serviettes, laminated menus with spelling mistakes, waiting staff in jeans and t-shirts, and a lower price tag. Both serve great food in a clean environment, just with different standards.

Next time you go into a restaurant, take a few minutes to try to understand at what level they've set their standards. How would your business stack up against your competitors in terms of service standards?

Grown-Up Businesses believe that "what gets measured gets done". If you don't know what's being done, you won't be able to make sure that it's being done to your standards, so you'll need to track and monitor your team's performance against your benchmarks. Without that, you'll never be able to ensure consistency and that's what a Grown-Up Business delivers every day. You need an early-warning system if standards are dropping so you can do something about it.

The feedback you gather is a rich vein of information. All this intelligence will ensure that your Grown-Up Business not only stays on track, but helps you spot opportunities both to improve the customer offering and to plug problem gaps. Your aim is two-fold:

- continuous improvement
- achieving consistency, consistently

If you study any business, you'll see that all of them have standards of some sort, but often they've developed over time and aren't consistent.

The Grown-Up Business works actively to deliver to its standards consistently. Take airlines, for example: Virgin and easyJet have clear standards. They may be very different standards, but what both airlines do extremely well is to deliver to those standards consistently, every time.

Standards must flow throughout the entire business, up, down, and sideways. Your role as the business owner is to set, with your team, the global standards that everyone in your organisation must follow without exception. Start them now and then drive implementation through so that they become second nature to everyone.

As you define your standards, this will inform your brand manifesto and vice versa. You'll embed the most crucial standards in your manifesto and these will also help you to develop the work house-rules.

One final reminder: if you offer a guarantee of any kind, then you will be judged on this every time. If you know you can deliver your product within 24 hours every time without exception, then that can be your guarantee or standard. But if you can only manage this 98% of the time, don't offer a 24-hour guarantee. Offer a 36-hour guarantee. You'll wow 98% of your customers and satisfy the 2%.

Many companies have a standards bible, albeit under many different names. Charlie Mullins developed a standards bible for Pimlico Plumbers when his business was struggling and he attributes his success, from that day on, to that. It hasn't changed much over the years but is extremely effective. Every employee is given one and everyone knows what is expected of them.

It details what they wear to work for both engineers and office employees. Every van is spotless and kept that way by an in-house team of valets. Every engineer is responsible for making sure the van has the correct spares. Engineers know that they take their shoes off at the customer's door every time, no exceptions, and they carry the hoover with them to the door. Every detail is covered.

Pimlico Plumbers are one of the most successful and profitable plumbers in London. They charge some of the highest prices, but another of their standards is to publish all their charge rates online, so every customer knows how much they have to pay – no nasty surprises. Why the success? It's because their standards are always the same. The service is consistently consistent and customers know what to expect, so they trust the brand and book a Pimlico plumber.

⮑ If you were your own customer, what would you want to see, hear, and feel every time you dealt with your company?
⮑ Ask your top three clients why they do business with you. What do they think you're really good at? What frustrates them when doing business with you?
⮑ Do your business standards hit the mark? Are you still aiming high or settling for mediocre?

Goal setting and objectives

If you don't know where you're going, you'll never get there. Without targets, you won't know where you're going, how you're progressing, whether you're getting close, missing the target or have achieved it already!

As soon as you set the target, though, expectations rise within your team, your customers, your investors. Publicly listed companies have to share their goals and objectives with the market analysts, shareholders, investors, and bankers. Depending on those goals and the company's ability to achieve them, these stakeholders will decide whether to continue to support the business or not. Effectively they hold the business to account. You're not forced to publish your goals to anyone, and there is no one to hold you to account unless you have borrowed money. So, it's down to you to set the goals, the time period and the budget, but most importantly it's your responsibility to make sure you achieve them.

Setting a goal allows you to focus on it completely. Look at Andy Murray's quest to win the Wimbledon Championship Men's Singles. It became a constant focus, sitting on his shoulder, dictating his actions. Your goal has you constantly asking, "If I do x, will it get me closer to achieving my goal?"

Footballers can't celebrate without scoring a goal and neither can you. Celebrations start once you achieve your target, but not until then. Celebrate, and then it's on to the next goal. Perhaps Andy Murray's next objective is to win Wimbledon again or to complete the Grand Slam.

Andy Murray's personal goals drive him and the money-making machine that is the Andy Murray brand. To fully understand and commit to the business goals, business owners must first consider their personal goals.

Personal goals

When was the last time you reflected on the past year, checked how you did against the goals you set yourself last year, or consciously set some new goals for the coming year? Did you just think about your business goals or did you consider your personal goals too? As a business owner, your personal goals should drive your business goals.

Patrick runs a successful insurance brokerage and has done for 28 years. He has clients that he's looked after for over 20 years. He loves his work – most of the time – and he's brilliant at what he does. He's making a good living but he also has time to play golf and take holidays. He'll never be a millionaire, but that isn't his goal.

Work-life balance is crucial – having time to see the kids while they're growing up, having time for other interests as well as playing golf. Yes, Patrick has his really busy times, those 20-hour days, but he can also make time for family, friends, and pastimes. Those are his personal objectives. Life's too short to be slaving away all day every day. His business goals focus on allowing him to also achieve his personal goals. To that end, he's built a great team, set up robust systems, and maintained a strong customer focus in the business. His reward is valuable time and the option to do his own thing when he wants to.

➲ Take 30 minutes now, right now, and think about your personal goals.

1 How much do you have to earn versus want to earn?
2 When do you want to retire, reduce your hours, or go part time?
3 Are you planning to sell the business or pass it onto the next generation?
4 How much time do you want to spend at work?
5 Is there something that you want to give back to the community?
6 How much time do you want for pastimes, holidays, downtime, etc?

Corporate goals

Now that you're clear about your own personal goals, it's time to review your business plan. Does it satisfy your personal goals? No? Then it's time to step back and review the plan to achieve your own goals. You might not be able to change this overnight, but start to make small changes now to get you to the end result within a reasonable time frame. Perhaps that means lots of hard work and hours now, with the pay-off in the future.

Just because you own a business, it doesn't mean you have to go for massive expansion or world domination. Sometimes, time, choice and a work-life balance is more important.

Corporate objectives are generally numbers based: £0000s turnover, £0000s profit, % market share, £0000s cash at bank. Those are the railway tracks inside which the business must operate. They are the benchmark against which all business decisions should be made. That question again: "If we do x, will that help us to achieve our corporate goals?" Don't forget that objectives and goals must be SMART: Specific, Measurable, Achievable, Relevant, and Targeted. Just a quick word on SMART. Over the years numerous words have been used for each letter. For example,

S could be stretching, specific, stated or specified and A, attainable or achievable. But for a goal to be really good it could be SMART, PURE (Positively stated, Understood, Relevant, Ethical) and CLEAR (Challenging, Legal, Environmental, Agreed, Recorded). The important part is to make sure that the goal you set is the right one!

Setting corporate goals also helps engage your team in achieving them. At the very least, if you actually tell them what they have to achieve, they will try. If they don't know what the goal is – both the actual target and the reason for it – they will lose focus and do their own thing.

Departmental goals naturally grow out of the corporate goals. If each department does its bit and hits its objectives, then the business should achieve the corporate objectives too.

The key to the success in departmental goals is that the department heads need to work across the business to match their goals with other departments, so that they all achieve the overall goal. For example, there's no point in the marketing department going ahead and launching the new product, if the production department can't make enough of it in time for the launch. It's great when a department hits an objective, but not at the expense of another department. Departmental egos have no place in a Grown-Up Business.

With the corporate objectives set and department goals in place, you can do a sense check across the business. Can you still achieve what you want to and by your target date? If no, it's back to the drawing board; if yes, it's time to start work.

Don't forget to record your progress so you know how you're doing. You'll need this to help you reforecast. If the business, industry, or economy shifts away from where you expect, you'll need to take this into account when you reforecast. If the objectives have to change too, then change them, but make sure everyone knows.

When I worked at Lloyds TSB (now the Lloyds Banking Group) in the late 90s, our corporate objectives were...

- to be the first choice for our customers
- reduce our expenses by x% every year
- be leaders in our chosen markets

Everything that we did – the new products designed and launched, new projects and initiatives, our day-to-day work – was mentally crosschecked against these three objectives. If it helped, we did it; if not, we stopped.

➲ Having set your personal goals, now establish your corporate goals. Most of these should focus on the numbers bit; profit, turnover, cash at bank, et cetera. But don't forget the big picture for your company:

1 Who do you want to be better than and why?
2 Which competitor would you like to buy and why?
3 Who would you like to buy your company?
4 How do you / should you behave towards your customers, employees and suppliers?
5 What can you give back to your community? What is your social responsibility?

➲ Once these are defined and in place, then make sure that the departmental, team, and individual goals or objectives are set.

Brand manifesto

In the good ol' days, textbooks and traditional business consultants told us that we had to have a mission statement; you weren't a proper business if you didn't have one. Most traditional businesses did have one. Many were ill-conceived, badly written and rarely implemented. These same thoughts extended to the vision statement. Vision statements should be something that everyone in the business can concentrate on and work towards, but in most cases, it was the business owner that dictated the vision, not the business or its customers.

Many businesses, in those good ol' days, also had a set of brand values. These were usually a series of words: professional, expert, reliable, value for money, ethical… The list goes on. I'm sure you'll recognise these from businesses you might have worked for, perhaps even your own.

Thankfully, the world has moved on. Our thinking has deepened, adjusted, and shifted. We think differently about how we operate, personally and as a business, about how we lead our people, and about why we do what we do. I'm pleased to say that the mission, vision, and values mindset has also shifted.

Many companies found the distinction between mission and vision statements far too confusing. They ended up with a set of meaningless, inward-looking statements, which took lots of time to develop and were communicated to everybody, but then were wholly ignored by everyone, including the leaders who had written them!

I discovered a wonderful alternative a few years ago: brand manifestos. I saw how they could be used to encompass the whole of the business in a freehand way that encourages creativity and personality, rather than the box-filling exercise that was the old mission, vision, and values statements. Manifestos, usually the preserve of political parties and organisations, don't have a wonderful reputation. They often come back to bite their owners hard on the bottom.

Despite this bad press, the private sector has adopted the manifesto principle and has turned them into living, breathing documents that showcase a business and keep everyone focused on the end goal.

A manifesto is a public declaration of policy. They work best when they're kept short. Think of it as a statement of intent, rather than the complete works of Shakespeare. The manifesto identifies what makes your company unique. It states why your brand does what it does. It articulates your core values and purpose. It can include whatever you like, but the best ones are made up of a series of words, statements, pictures or phrases. Consider…

- a set of principles that you believe in
- words that inspire you, your customers, and your employees
- statements such as "we believe", "we choose", "we think", "we want", and "we do"
- "thou shalt" statements, such as "Thou shalt know our staff, our suppliers, our customers, and our costs."

Essentially, the manifesto is an inspiring précis of your business. It's a way of inspiring both customers and staff. Customers have generally stopped caring about vague aspirations. They want to be inspired by your brand; they want to understand your beliefs, rules, and goals. They want to engage with your authentic and unique experience.

Manifestos have no standard formats, words, or phrases. Every word means something, is there for a reason, and is spoken from the heart. You'll see that several manifestos also include "no", "won't" or "don't" statements – what the company will not do, will not get involved with, will not tolerate. These are an integral part of the manifesto, alongside your goals, so you'll need to include both.

You'll find many examples of fantastically brilliant corporate manifestos online. Each one is unique. My current favourite is Frog Design (www. frogdesign.com):

We are fanatical about IMPROVING THE WORLD. We strive to change minds, touch hearts, and move markets. Our passion is to transform ideas INTO realities. QUALITY IS OUR NON-COMPROMISING OBLIGATION. WE ARE CURIOUS, VIGILANT, expert, co$t-driven, AND AWARE of the need to save our scarce environment. OUR TALENT IS BOTH AN ART & A SCIENCE. It is both business and culture. OUR CLIENTS ARE THE KEY TO OUR SUCCESS. *However, we don't take any b.s. —inside or outside. WE LIVE HONESTLY, OPEN AND WITHOUT FEAR. HUMOR AND SPIRITED FUN ARE THE ESSENCE OF FROG.

So how do you start your manifesto? Easy.

- ⮐ Jot down your beliefs and key words or phrases about you and your business; see what develops. Write down whatever comes into your head – you're gathering random thoughts now.
- ⮐ For a few days, mull over what you've written down and add to the list as other thoughts ping on like light bulbs. You can refine it and then finalise it later.
- ⮐ Ask others what they think of your business; ask your staff and customers what's important about what you do and how you do it. Mull it over: let your subconscious take over first and then refine it later. There are no rules. Be creative; develop something you passionately believe in that inspires others.
- ⮐ Set aside half an hour. Get yourself a pen, paper, and a glass of your favourite beverage, and make sure you're not disturbed.
- ⮐ If you need some inspiration, just type "inspiring brand manifesto" into your search engine and prepare to be amazed.

Work house-rules

Sitting alongside your brand manifesto and your standards are the work house-rules. Remove the word "work" and you'll probably understand what I mean. Households have house rules: be in by 10 o'clock, lock the doors, turn out the lights when you're not in the room, keep your bedroom tidy, dirty washing goes in the bin, not on the floor, put your dirty cup straight in the dishwasher….

In the workplace, the work house-rules are the rules by which every member of the team should behave. They aren't found in the job description or the contract of employment but they should find a place in your staff handbook. They are the guidelines for behaviour, attitude and habits in your business. They document exactly what is expected of each person. This is the "how to behave at work while achieving objectives" bit. They can be used at staff appraisal time, as well as in one-to-ones that you have with your team. I'm a firm believer that if you don't tell your team what is expected of them, what you want them to do, and how they should behave, then they will do what they like when they like and chaos will reign.

Work house-rules are an important part of being a Grown-Up Business, but they'll only work if you, as the boss, live them too. You have to follow them to the letter. If you don't, then why would your team? You can't have double standards, ever. You also have to have a penalty for non-compliance: you have to commit to policing them.

If you're a start-up, you can start these rules from day one. If you have an existing business, you'll need to change behaviours and quickly. All my clients now have their own set of work house-rules, although they're called different things to suit each business. The template is the same, but the execution is specific and unique to each business. They have been written, implemented, and adopted (almost universally) by their teams.

As you might expect, some team members are dragging their heels in the adoption process. They've been spotted by the boss and their colleagues. Very soon, they'll either fall in line gracefully, be pulled into line by colleagues, or leave the business. Whatever the outcome, it'll be a good one for the business.

Here are two examples of work house-rules. The first is taken from Nigel Botterill's book, *The Botty's Rules*, where work house-rules are called "What it's like to work here?" The second is taken from Sam Carpenter's book, *Work the System*.

What's it like to work here...?

We work a fair and full day
This means that time at work is spent productively! Personal stuff needs to be kept to a minimum, this includes taking personal calls, sending texts, checking Facebook or chatting on twitter or MSN!

We are a team
We're in this together. Being in a team means that it is never "not my job".

We're proud of our work
Because we take pride in the work we do, we do it as it is intended to be done. No shortcuts, omissions, bodge-jobs or work-arounds. We will support every employee who does deliver a fair, just, and full day of compliant work, by not saddling them with the slack of any bad employees.

We respect our customers

They pay our wages and are the reason for our existence. We always seek to understand them to see things from their point of view and we never slag them off.

We keep our promises

When we say we'll do something or we'll get back to someone, we do it. We don't let people down – colleagues, customers or suppliers.

We're positive

It's not okay to say negative things about the company or any of our customers or staff. We won't tolerate – at all – anything or anyone that contributes negative word of mouth.

We don't do things slowly

We do them quickly or not at all. This means that there'll always be lots going on – and things will change as we adapt and spot new opportunities. It's never been calm around here and as long as we're successful it never will be!

We're in business to make a profit

We're not here for fun. Getting and keeping customers is the most important thing we do. Creating profit is fundamental to any successful company and the people we value most are the ones that contribute to profit.'

It's not enough to be busy; as teams and as individuals, we need to ask ourselves "what are we busy doing?" If you are not focusing on profit, you're doing something wrong. It's okay for anybody to question anybody else, at any time, about what they're doing and how it contributes to profit.

We finish stuff

Our key measures of success and performance will be based around what you got done, not what you are doing. We don't like activity masquerading as accomplishment – you need to focus on getting things done. Not "doing" or "in the pipeline" but properly done; finished; crossed off. Achieved!

We recognise and reward good thinking
We can all find better more efficient ways to do stuff – and we've all got a responsibility to speak up and share those thoughts.

We think before we act
Making an honest mistake when you've thought something through and did it for the right reasons. In fact it's encouraged. However, doing something dumb because you didn't think is unforgiveable.

We don't clock watch
Working at N5 means putting in some extra hours – this isn't "face-time" – we do it because we enjoy working here and we believe in what we're doing.

We work hard, play hard and eat lunch
At lunch time we get out of the office. Eating at our desks is an exception, not the rule. We all need breaks to work effectively,

We keep our workplace clean and tidy
Everything should have a home – we don't let stuff congregate by desks, stairs or corridors

Reproduced from Botty's Rules *book by kind permission of Nigel Botterill.* *www.nigelbotterill.com*

Centratel's 30 Principles

1   Company decisions must conform to the Strategic Objective, 30 Principles, and Working Procedure documents.
2   We are the highest-quality answering service in the United States. We do whatever it takes to make sure the quality of service to our clients is unmatched anywhere.
3   We draw solid lines, thus providing an exact status of where things stand. Documented procedures are the main defense against gray-area problems.
4   "Get the job done." Can the employee do his or her job, or is there always a complication of one kind or another? This ability to "get the job done quickly and accurately without excuses or complications," is the most valuable trait an employee can possess.

5   Employees come first. We employ people who have an innate desire to perform at 100 percent. We reward them accordingly. The natural outcome is that we serve our clients well.

6   We are not fire-killers. We are fire prevention specialists. We don't manage problems; we work on system-improvements and system-maintenance to prevent problems from happening in the first place.

7   Problems are gifts that inspire us to action. A problem prompts the act of creating or improving a system or procedure. We don't want setbacks, but when one occurs, we think, "thank you for this wake-up call," and take system-improvement action to prevent the setback from happening again.

8   We focus on just a few manageable services. Although we watch for new opportunities, in the end we provide "just a few services implemented in superb fashion," rather than a complex array of average-quality offerings.

9   We find the simplest solution. Ockham's Law, also called the Law of Economy, states, "Entities are not to be multiplied beyond necessity…the simplest solution is invariably the correct solution."

10   The money we save or waste is not Monopoly money. We are careful not to devalue the worth of a dollar just because it has to do with the business.

11   We operate the company via documented procedures and systems. "Any recurring problem can be solved with a system." We must take the time to create and implement systems and procedures, but in the end, it is well worth it. Our staff must know what management expects and if there is a recurring problem, a written procedure must be created to stop that problem from happening again. On the other hand, we don't bog down the organization with systems and procedures that target once-in-a-while problems. Sometimes we elect to not create a procedure.

12   "Just don't do it." Eliminate the unnecessary. Think simplicity. Automate. Refine to the smallest amount of steps or discard altogether. Would a simple "no" save time, energy, and/or money? Sometimes, elimination of a system, protocol, or potential project is a good thing.

13   Our documented systems, procedures, and functions are "off the street." This means that anyone with normal intelligence can perform procedures unassisted. The real-world evidence of this is we can hire an individual "off the street" who has good

typing skills, and have him or her processing calls within three days. Before we implemented our systemized training protocol, it would take six weeks to train a TSR. For this result, systems have to be efficient, simple, and thoroughly documented.

14 Do it NOW. All actions build on "point-of-sale" theory. We don't delay an action if it can be done immediately. Just like any major retail outlet, we "update inventories and databases at the exact time the transaction takes place." There is no paperwork floating around the office after a physical transaction. We ask, "How can we perform the task NOW without creating lingering details that we must clean up later?"

15 We glean the Centratel mindset from Steven Covey's books including *The 7 Habits of Highly Successful People, First Things First,* and *The Eighth Habit.* As well, we consider *From Good to Great* by Jim Collins; *The E-Myth Revisited* by Michael Gerber, and *Release the Giant Within* by Tony Robbins.

16 We pattern personal organization upon Franklin Covey theory. We use personal organizing systems that are always at hand. We prioritize, schedule, and document. The system is always up-to-date and we use it all the time. (For Centratel, this system is Microsoft Outlook).

17 Sequence is critical. We work on the most important tasks first. We spend maximum time on "non-urgent/important" tasks via Steven Covey's time-matrix philosophy.

18 We double-check everything before its release. If a penchant for double-checking is not an innate personal habit, then it must be cultivated. Double-checking is a conscious step in every task, performed either by the individual managing the task, or someone else.

19 Our environment is spotless: clean and ordered, simple, efficient, functional. No "rat's nests," literally or figuratively.

20 Employee training is structured, scheduled, and thorough. Assertive client contact is also structured, scheduled, and thorough.

21 We are deadline-obsessed. If someone in the organization says they will be finished with a task or project by a certain date and time, then he or she commits to finishing by that deadline (or, if legitimate delays intrude, advises their co-worker well in advance that the deadline is impossible).

22 We maintain equipment and keep it 100 percent functional at all times. If something is not working as it should, fix it now -

fix it now even if it's not necessary to fix it now. It's a matter of good housekeeping and of maintaining good habits. This is just the way we do things.

23 Mastery of the English language is critical. We are aware of how we sound and what we write. We do whatever we can to improve. We are patient as a co-worker corrects us.

24 We study to increase our skills. A steady diet of reading and contemplation is an important part of personal and job self-development. It is a matter of self-discipline.

25 As opposed to "doing the work," the department manager's job is to create, monitor, and document systems (which consist of people, equipment, procedures, and maintenance schedules).

26 The CEO/General Manager oversees department heads and systems. It is the CEO/GM's job to direct, coordinate, and monitor the entire operation.

27 We avoid multi-tasking activities. When communicating with someone else, we are 100 percent present. We give full attention to the person in front of us. We focus on listening and understanding. Read the classic *Treating Type A Behavior and Your Heart* by Meyer Friedman. "Mindfulness" is paying complete attention to one thing at a time: Read *Full Catastrophe Living* by Jon Kabat-Zinn.

28 When in the office, we work hard on Centratel business. We keep our heads down; we focus, and, in turn, the company pays very well. That's "the deal." The workweek is a maximum of 40 - 45 hours.

29 "Complete" means complete. "Almost" or "tomorrow" is not "complete." In particular, this is germane to administration staff's use of Outlook task functions.

30 This can't be legislated, but we strive for a social climate that is serious and quiet, yet pleasant, serene, light, and friendly. Centratel is a nice place to work.

Reproduced from Work The System, The Simple Mechanics of Making more and Working Less *by Sam Carpenter, www.workthesystem.com.*

A friend of mine worked in a processing centre for a large clearing bank. Her hours were from 9 am to 5 pm and, as you can imagine, all their work was IT-based. They all knew that they had to work until 5 pm, not leave the building at 5 pm. If they logged off their computer before 5 pm, they were docked 15 minutes' pay.

A client of mine had four staff working five days a week for the same hours: 9 am to 5 pm. However, his staff were out the door at 5 pm sharp. They logged off early, probably at 4:50 pm, had a chat, packed up their desk, put their coats on, and walked out bang on 5 pm and not a minute later. That was all fine if that was what was expected of the staff, but I know he didn't intend that. By ignoring this early finish, he was losing five hours of production a week. The same was happening at the start of the day, too: they walked into the office at 9 am and probably don't start work until 9:15. That made 10 hours a week of lost production – a third of one salary that he was losing. He used the work house-rules as a basis to change their behaviour and for him to regain those lost hours each week.

How do you develop a set of rules that everyone understands and embraces? To implement them successfully, you need to get your team involved early in the process. It always amazes me that when you get the team to come up with the work house-rules, they set much tougher rules than they'd accept if they'd been given them! Writing your rules in isolation and imposing them on your team won't work very well. This is my route map:

- Explain what you want to achieve and why.
- Get the staff involved as early as possible.
- Ask them for suggestions. A team meeting and a 10-minute brainstorming session will highlight lots of aspects. Once you have an outline list, then you can start to refine it.
- Prepare a first draft for comments from the team.
- Give your team time to work on them, discuss, debate, and write them.
- You'll soon have their buy-in, commitment, and enthusiasm.

As you go through this process, you'll start to think more about the staff attributes that your team already have and notice those who don't really fit. You'll need either to get them to change their attitude or to look at leaving the business. One bad apple will soon sour the box.

Once the work house-rules are in place, your staff will uphold them, so allow them to police the rules as well – not aggressively but helpfully. You'll quickly find that they won't tolerate bad behaviour and peer pressure can be a powerful tool.

Once your team is pulling in the same direction with the right behaviours, you can use the work house-rules in your recruitment process. How will prospective employees adopt and live the rules? In the first interview, score each candidate against your work house-rules list – remember that you're not just recruiting for skills, but for attitude and habit too. Circulate the list to interviewees before the second interview, and get them to comment on the work house-rules as part of your selection process.

- ➲ As the business owner you have to initiate the work house-rules. Take half an hour to make a start by jotting down some of your own rules.
- ➲ Now set up a working party or cross-functional team and work through the route map above.

Write it down

The brain is a wonderful thing. It's amazing just how much we can remember, but it's frightening just how much we forget. I have so many ideas, thoughts, and things to do whizzing into my head in a random order that remembering them is a real challenge. The only way I have found to overcome these tendencies is to write it down, but I also need to access it easily sometime in the future. I've become a great list writer. I reprioritise my list regularly. It goes everywhere with me and any minute I get to act on something, I do.

I know that having a second brain helps. In Graham Allcott's excellent book, *How to Be a Productivity Ninja*, he explains how our brains work more productively when we allow a second brain to store information. This frees up the first one for valuable thinking. It may sound like cheating to use a storage device but wow is it effective. There are four reasons to write something down:

1 to not forget it, a reminder to do…
2 to understand it, to sort it out, to learn it, to cut it down
3 to remember it, a reference point, a why, a record of what we thought – a diary
4 to clear your head, to identify what you want, to set out your intentions

When you write anything down, it becomes real, not just a thought. Only when you have written it down can you refer back to it and check to see how you've done. Whether it's list-writing, mindmapping, daybook-using, or Post-it noting, find a system that works for you, because writing it down will help.

Just as we write our to-do lists, so we must also write down our goals, ambitions, and objectives for them to become real. Your business plan and forecast becomes a combination of your objectives and your to-do list – sometimes it might be called your action plan.

I see far too many business plans that would prop a door open. In fact, that's all they're good for. Yes, you learn a lot while you're writing the business plan, although it takes a huge amount of time to write the perfect plan. But the minute you have to search in the plan for something specific, you've lost.

There is a place in business for these large business plans and that's when you're seeking either debt (a bank loan) or equity (money for shares) investment. Investors will want to see chapter and verse, even though they'll generally only read the one-page executive summary at the front and the financial forecast at the back. (But what about the little gems hidden in the pages in between? Your role is to pull them into the executive summary.)

The main problem with a huge business plan is that it is hard to "make it live". How many times have you been given a 25-page report on something, only to read the first few pages thoroughly and then skim through the rest? How many times have you had to physically highlight the good bits in the text or make your own shorthand notes so that you don't forget? How much easier would it be to read one page of quality bullet points and notes which give you all the vital information? Now isn't your executive summary effectively a one-page plan?

Instead of long waffly paragraphs, think bullet points and short sentences. A bulleted list of say five to seven points can save many paragraphs of rambling words. I advocate one-page plans for everything. They're…

- quick to read and write, so more likely to be achieved
- easier to understand because they use simpler language
- better at keeping everybody engaged
- easier to communicate
- prompts for discussion and debate

You might need a series of one-page plans and that's fine, just don't break the one-page habit. A colleague of mine says that if you can't communicate it on one page, either you've no chance of selling it or you don't have a clue yourself! Harsh but true.

You already have your goals and objectives list, your brand manifesto, the work house-rules, and your standards document. Each of these should only be one page. There are three additional pieces of paper that you need to run your business:

1 a one-page business plan: the executive summary
2 a business and cash-flow forecast: the spreadsheet with the numbers bit (more information on that in chapter 8)
3 a calendar, preferably a large one stuck on the wall

I recently worked with a firm of consulting surveyors who needed help to kickstart their business: growth had stagnated and was starting to decline. They were very proud of their business plans and sent me copies: they almost crashed my inbox! The business plan was 76 pages long; the marketing plan a similar length. The financial forecast was just three pages, one for each year. What a blessing!

It was all great stuff: a huge amount of work and thought had gone into it and it all made sense. It was just so long – not a bullet point or numbered list in sight. The problem was that the plan was two and a half years old.

From the day it was written, it had propped the door open. It was never implemented, reviewed, or reforecast. Why? Because it was a major feat just to read the thing. It wasn't action-orientated and didn't talk to the team in their language. It didn't answer the "why" question for the staff. It was never updated because it became such a daunting job to rewrite, edit, and review all 76 pages. Now if it had been a one-page plan it would have been a different story.

They were adamant that they shouldn't or couldn't proceed without a fully up-to-date and comprehensive plan. But I knew that if they embarked on the 76 page version we would never get anything implemented that would reverse decline and help the business to start growing. It was hard work persuading them to let go of the comfort blanket, which the big plan had become and to trust the one-page plan.

We prepared the plan, the calendar, and the financial forecast for the next 12 months. It didn't take very long: all the hard work had been done in the previous plan. The gems were there; we just needed to pull them out onto one page and reassess them. We wrote it, finalised it, and tested it against the SMART rules. Then we communicated it to the team. They loved it. It was clear, concise, understandable, and didn't take them long to read but was full of valuable signposts. Using the one-page plan, each department and team could create their own action plans to deliver the objectives.

Now that the team knew both what they had to achieve and why, things started to happen. Objectives were achieved, confidence grew alongside job satisfaction, and smiles started to return and grow too. Clients noticed and bought more, clients that had drifted away started to return, and new clients came knocking on their door.

They now held their monthly performance reviews against the plan instead of cancelled them. Progress sped up, once everyone was now contributing. Reforecasting became much easier and more enjoyable, especially as the numbers started to climb. The business now has a clear concise one-page plan that the team are implementing and successes are coming in.

Here's my list of headings for your one-page business plan:

Our Goal: Two lines here

Our Objectives: Just a bullet point

Financial

Markets

People

Products

For example:
- *Increase average order value by 7.5% all sales to existing customers*
- *Double / treble sales of products A & B in X and Y countries/regions*
- *Develop additional and alternative products to use same distribution model*
- *Reduce debt level to £x by 20XX*

Our Key Markets: Current / planned, home or export

Our Key Customer Segments: Current & future

Our Key Products: Growing, declining, in development, with assets such as patents or licences; key growth areas and margins

Our Key Competitors: Current & future market

Financial Priorities: a couple of lines or few bullets

KPIs: what are they, when they're measured

Key actions for next period: a few key points

To help people's initial understanding, you might also want to include a few appendices, but keep each one to just a page:

1 The Internal or Micro or 4Ms Audit reviews in detail the internal environment of your company. The 4Ms being Men, Money, Machinery, Methods. Here you assess the good and the bad and use the audit findings to determine what you need to improve.

2 The External or Macro Audit is focused on the external environment. It uses letters to remind you what areas to review. PESTLE Analysis is the most common and is Political, Economic, Social, Technology, Legal and Environmental. These are the external influences that you have little control over but which could make a major impact, positive or negative, on your business.

3 SWOT Analysis: Strengths, Weaknesses, Opportunities and Threats. SWOT analysis is very versatile; it can be used on a business, a project, a product – in fact, almost anything. It's worth taking time to think about each step of the SWOT analysis carefully; too many businesses rush this model and miss the real benefits. How can we emphasise our Strengths and compensate for our Weaknesses? How do we maximise our Opportunities and protect ourselves against Threats?

4 The Boston Consulting Group (BCG) growth / share matrix was developed in 1970 to review and assess products. It's a great tool to help you start the strategy planning process and gives a visual representation of your products, showing which products you need to focus your attention on. The four grouping are generally called stars, cash cows, problem children, and dogs.

5 A Product Life Cycle (PLC) Analysis helps you to map out in a diagram where each of your products or product ranges are in their life cycle. The life cycle is a curve plotting its Introduction, Adoption, Growth, Maturity and Decline.

6 Knowing what your competitors are doing is an important part of your planning and strategy development. Competitor Analysis is a systematic assessment of factors that apply to your business and that of your competitors. This might include such factors as product quality, delivery, premises, pricing, and brand strength. The key is to assess your company and all of your competitors against each factor to glean an overall picture. It gives the strengths and weaknesses of both your current and potential competitors.

7 Market Share Analysis is used to establish exactly how much business you and your competitors have or control in the market. Many business commentators believe that increasing market share is an important objective.

➲ Whether or not you already have a business plan, print this business plan template out at www.grownupbusiness.com/extras and complete it blind first, as a test. Only then go back through your existing business records or existing plan and see what you missed.

➲ If you've already written a business plan, then get it out, dust it off, grab yourself a highlighter pen, and work through it. Highlight the little gems as you go and scribble notes of changes that you need to make since the last plan. With the headings from the one-page plan in mind, take the valuable little gems out of your big plan and insert them into your one-page plan.

➲ Share the new formatted plan with everyone.

➲ Ask them to ask you questions, so you'll find out what you have missed.

Problems crop up: deal with them now

Businesses that lurch from one problem to another have only one way to go: down. At best, they manage to stay afloat, but the stress and worry take their toll on the boss and the team. Conversely, a company that grabs the problem by the scruff of the neck and solves it will make more money, grow sustainably, and have fun. Life is just so much better that way – the victor rather than the victim.

You can never allow problems to undermine your standards, ever. Anything that stops you hitting an objective or damages the customer's experience in any way is not acceptable to a Grown-Up Business.

A problem is anything that disrupts the status quo. A quick example: I'm offered a choice of tea or coffee and choose tea, only to be told that they've run out of tea. If I'd only been offered coffee, I would've accepted that, but my taste buds are after tea now! The fact that there is no tea is disruptive. I feel let down, they feel embarrassed, and someone has to go to the shops! It disrupts the customer experience and it undermines your standards.

Customers dislike…

- incompetence
- inconvenience
- inconsistency
- being ignored, forgotten, or taken for granted
- inefficiency or waste

When a customer experiences one or more of these dislikes, they walk away from your business as a customer – and then they tell everyone else how bad you were.

Committing to solving problems is a standard you have to set. The whole of chapter 9 addresses problem solving; it's that critical. For now, suffice to say that failing to solve a real problem costs the business time, money, and effort – all valuable resources that shouldn't be wasted.

That doesn't mean you never have problems. However brilliant your business and your people are, problems do crop up. Grown-Up Businesses will…

- deal with the complaint as soon as possible to the customer's complete satisfaction
- solve the real problem as soon as possible
- test thoroughly that the problem is really fixed
- use the opportunity to make the customer experience even better than it was
- make sure the same problem never happens again

I recently had some gunky stuff pumped into my tyres to prevent a puncture if I hit a nail. My husband and daughter also had it done to their cars. Theirs were fine, but mine wasn't. The steering wheel shaking at 50 mph was a bit worrying! I called the gunk guys. They suggested that I took a few roundabouts at speed (at night, of course) and did some figure-of-eight movements in a large car park, to splosh the gunky stuff up the sides of the tyre. No joy.

I had to take the car back and wait for the gunk to be washed out of the tyres. I arrived at a time that suited me; they opened early and had the coffee pot on. They explained that the inside moulding of the tyre might be causing the problem and asked if I'd like to try another solution. As expected (it always happens to me), my tyres had grooves on the inside, which meant the gunky stuff couldn't stick to the tyre, making it unstable.

They held up their hands, admitting that they'd discovered that some low-profile tyres are a problem. They reassured me that they'd taken steps to avoid it happening again. In short, they'd rectified the mistake as soon as I gave them the opportunity, making me a happy bunny.

- ➲ Set a standard in your company now to deal with a problem as soon as you discover it.
- ➲ Commit to using every problem to make the customer experience even better than it was before.
- ➲ Take a walk through your customer experience. How would you feel the first, second, or fiftieth time you bought your product or service?
- ➲ Take one issue and solve it now: make it better.

Why processes and systems matter

Without necessarily recognising it, we have processes and systems for just about everything we do – drawing cash from an ATM, starting the car, packing a suitcase, or cooking a roast dinner. All of our processes have become habits over the years. Milk or tea in the cup first? Whichever you prefer, you'll do it that way every time. In his book *Work the System*, Sam Carpenter takes changing the toilet roll as his process example: it's hilarious! So if our daily lives are run according to our own processes, why don't our businesses run on such a process-driven basis?

Documented processes will really strengthen the value of your business when you come to sell it, but they also deliver significant value while you're still running it. I've talked several times already about consistency. This is one of the biggest differentiators between Grown-Up Businesses and the rest. Customers are comfortable with consistent service; they dislike inconsistency of any kind. The only way to achieve a consistent customer experience is to have documented processes that everyone follows, every time. Don't think that you can have undocumented processes held in someone's head. That won't work on any level, least of all consistency. And the day that person gets ill or leaves, you'll have trouble!

Whatever your view of franchises, they are scalable businesses because they have a complete set of documented processes for everything. As well as a visible brand that grows with each franchisee, the big advantage they have over a start-up is their tried and tested processes. Those fully documented processes are one of the main items that you buy when you sign on the dotted line for your franchise.

In *The E-Myth Revisited*, Michael Gerber focuses on systematising a business as the only way for a business to break free of the day to day and the only real sustainable way to scale it. Two million burgers with ketchup and mustard is the same as 200 or 2000, if the process is scalable.

Simply designing a process and putting it in place isn't enough. Continual process refinement is the Grown-Up Business approach. Encourage your team to suggest ways of enhancing processes, to make them quicker, better, cheaper, and more robust. Customer complaints will reduce over time as your consistency improves, but in the early days use those complaints to help you define and redefine the processes.

Always start with processes that impact the customer. Concentrate on those until you have a consistently robust process which benefits the customer. Your business will naturally benefit from that. Think about ordering, product returns, dispatch and delivery, packaging, upselling, customer queries, invoicing, and payment processes.

Your brand manifesto and standards document is a great source of inspiration in defining the processes. Make sure that your processes match up with the expectations you've set in your brand manifesto.

Teams need to develop their processes alongside each other, not in isolation from the rest of the business. For example, in the sales process, you'll need a credit check for any new account customer. Therefore, sales and the accounts teams must work together to ensure that...

- credit checks aren't overlooked
- credit checks don't hold up or bottleneck the sales process
- the credit check outcome is communicated to the right people and computer systems
- it's included in the client file and the customer ordering system
- everyone knows that the credit check will be done again in three months' time

Once you've developed the process with your team, you'll have a master set of processes that run throughout the whole of your business. Your role will be managing the processes, because that way your team will start to manage themselves. You'll work on these processes to improve them, track them, and keep them documented. It will take some time to fully document your whole business, but the sooner you start, the sooner you'll start to see the benefits:

- Do you need that expensive, skilled person to put mustard and ketchup in the burger or could you employ a lower-cost person, saving you money?
- The processes become a readymade
  o training manual
  o job description
  o performance monitor
- Someone who used to do the role can induct staff rather than an expensive manager.
- You reduce wastage (back to the ketchup and mustard!).
- It's easier to cover holidays as anyone can step in and cover that role by just following the processes.

If each person knows what's expected of them and when they need to do it, they will. If your team are left to their own devices, chaos starts to take over and customers become disenchanted with your inconsistent approach.

From the start, set out a central control system. Keep the documented processes in the same place in the same format. Agree who approves the processes in the first place, who can amend them, and how the new version is stored. Cloud computing with computer files is ideal: everyone has the latest version all the time and no old paper versions muddy the waters.

The rules of processes

1 Every process is documented.
2 Every document has the same format and is stored in the same place.
3 Every process has a review date and it's reviewed.
4 No one has the monopoly on a good idea.

Let's return to franchises. If you're not convinced, think of McDonald's. It's by far the best-known and most successful franchise operation and that's wholly due to the operational manual that's been developed and improved over many years. Nothing is left to chance. There's a process for everything and it's been tested to destruction. It's regularly reviewed and refined to make it even better. There's even a process on how to add mustard and ketchup to a burger. Why?

- It's designed so that the customer gets a taste of both mustard and ketchup with each mouthful.
- The ketchup and mustard doesn't spurt out of the side of the burger bun all over people's hands or clothes.
- Portion control is precise: not too much mustard to burn your mouth, but enough to get a good taste.
- Because every portion is the same, there's no wastage ever and costs are strictly controlled.
- Anyone can put mustard and ketchup in a burger correctly if they follow the process.

But most of all you get the same result, whether it's the second burger, the second thousandth, or the second million. The customer gets the same every time, no exceptions. It's a consistent experience, one that they will buy again and again.

With good systems and processes, everybody knows what to do and when. Your whole business, just like McDonald's, can be systematised to give you this consistency. When every process has been documented, tested, and refined, you'll have ironed out the creases, filled the gaps in your service, and smoothed out the customer experience.

In chapter 7, we'll look in more detail at documenting every process in the business. Right now, though, you're going to pick just one activity and turn it into a process.

- ➲ Think about one thing that you do regularly. Write down the steps you go through in the order that you do them.
- ➲ Have you broken it down into individual activities, instead of grouping bits together? Congratulations! You have now written a process.
- ➲ Now find someone else to test it, to see if it works. 80% don't work the first time!
- ➲ Ask them to suggest improvements, then test it again until it works. You have effectively delegated that task to a cheaper person.

We've covered lots in this chapter, but if you get these basics in place right now, you're well on your way to becoming a Grown-Up Business. The key with all of them is consistency. If you're consistent, then customers will love you and come back repeatedly. Employees will know what to do, when to do it, and how to do it, but above all will understand why it has to be done a certain way.

As the business owner, you're the one who sets these basics in place and you also have to live by the same rules every day. If you want your entire team to adopt your standards, be consistent yourself!

Chapter 6

Do Something Different and Make More Money

Grown-Up Businesses are often described as being "innovative", but what exactly does that mean? Lots of people assume innovation is all about coming up with creative, wacky, off-the-wall product ideas. But it's not all about the products, or "crazy" creativity – it's much more than that. I love this explanation, from the Australian government website: "Innovation generally refers to reviewing, changing or creating more effective processes, products or ways of doing things."

Innovation is about the whole business, not just products, and a Grown-Up Business takes innovation into everything it does. One of my past bosses and now a mentor of mine has a great phrase for innovation: "Do something different and make more money."

Do something different is about making a change. Sometimes that's a temporary change, such as handling an unexpected influx of orders or coping with a huge snowfall. Sometimes it's a permanent change or improvement, such as a new manufacturing process or a replacement component made of better material. Ultimately, you're aiming for permanent improvement.

Doing something different *to make more money* means that the something different has to be the *right* different. Hold fire before you start changing everything. Change for change's sake is not the goal here. You want to become constantly alert to what *has to* change. The question to ask yourself is, "How can this be better, quicker, easier, and cheaper?"

Let's start doing something different and making more money. In this chapter, we're going to consider seven approaches where you can make vast improvements to the running of your business, which will revolutionise how your business operates and how you can make money.

Moments of truth

How disappointed do you feel when a supplier lets you down? The product or service you've ordered doesn't arrive on time or is just such poor quality. You have an emotional reaction: frustrated, stressed, disenchanted. That emotional response affects how you see that supplier; you might reconsider whether you'll use them again. This is called a moment of truth.

A bad moment of truth is when something goes wrong. You also have good (or great) moments of truth occur when everything runs smoothly and the company meets or exceeds your expectations. You're happy to continue the relationship, because it was a good experience for the money you paid.

A moment of truth is a point in time when the customer...

- interacts with the supplier
- has an emotional reaction of some kind, good or bad
- makes a decision about that supplier as a result of their experience

A Grown-Up Business understands that its customers have multiple moments of truth throughout their relationship with the business. It recognises that it also has moments of truth with its suppliers that impact on the business, positively or negatively. The challenge for a Grown-Up Business is to eliminate the bad moments of truth and make sure that every moment of truth a customer has is good. Likewise, it needs to manage its moments of truth with its suppliers, to keep everything flowing smoothly.

Customers

How do your customers feel when your company fails to deliver on time or sends an inferior product? Just the same emotions as you do when a supplier lets you down. They might complain to you and if they do, that's a good response – at least you then get a chance to correct the problem and go on to wow them! More likely, though, they'll simply walk away from doing business with you in the future. What is almost certain is they will share their bad experience with lots of other people. Your brand is damaged: you've almost certainly lost at least one customer and in turn several other prospects might not do business with you, because of what they've heard about you.

Let's flip the coin, now. Your customer has a great experience using your company. Not only have you sent the right product on time, but it works brilliantly. It arrives in good condition and it's a great price. How does your customer react? They come back to you for more of the same. They tell everyone how great you are. They check what else you can supply for them, since they loved the experience so much. They write a great review or give you a testimonial.

Grown-Up Businesses understand that moments of truth impact the business. They work hard to keep their customers happy, by ensuring that the customers get a good moment of truth every time.

If you offer guarantees on service, product availability, delivery times, and so on, remember that these offers will set up extra moments of truth in the customer's mind. "Order by 5 pm and receive your product the next day" is a great offer – but consider the customer's emotional reaction if it doesn't arrive!

Suppliers

Where a Grown-Up Business stands head and shoulders above other companies is that they take moments of truth to another level: they use the exact same philosophy with their suppliers. By doing so, they add even better results for both their business and their customers. They don't accept the increased costs and lost time if they're badly treated by their supplier. They understand that they have a choice: either change supplier and solve the problem that way, or take a grown-up approach and address the issue directly with the supplier to develop a robust solution to the problem. They save time and money, plus the business is guaranteed a much more consistent service in the future, which helps everyone.

Imagine you run ABC Printing Supplies Ltd, supplying printing plates to printers all over the world. You source your products from three manufacturers and then distribute the plates to your clients, using efficient logistics, couriers, and haulage contractors. Imagine the frustration, delay, and cost if the manufacturers deliver whenever they think fit and not when the deliveries are scheduled! They turn up late, miss the delivery slots at your warehouse, and sometimes all arrive at the same time. Now it's your problem – a bad moment of truth and wow are you having a bad emotional reaction! This is the impact for you:

You spend extra time and therefore money chasing outstanding deliveries. This unpredictability means that you need to hold more product in stock, just in case they don't deliver in time. This ties up your working capital (cash). Furthermore, you need more storage space, which is an extra cost.

You need extra resources. Maybe you end up with three lorries of deliveries all arriving at exactly the same time. Doubtless that's just when your courier arrives to collect your customer shipments. Suddenly you need twice as many people in the warehouse. That means that you might have to go out to help, but remember: you cost the business £59 per hour. Not only is it disruptive, it's expensive.

You can't plan everything and everyone is stressed. Resource planning is virtually impossible.

When they do deliver, you often find that only part of the order arrives. Every delivery has to be double-checked. You might discover a "part order" that you now have to deal with: extra cost, lost time, and even more frustration.

The manufacturer's invoices follow the orders placed, not what's been delivered. It now takes the accounts team a lot of extra time to agree invoices for payment. Your warehouse team has to deal with another delivery. The sales team don't really know what's in stock, to confirm a sale to a customer, without a lot of double-checking!

One particular product often arrives damaged; the packaging isn't good enough. You have to return it or hold on to it until the manufacturer next delivers, whenever that may be. Now you have to request a credit note or replacement products. Ouch, that costs you a lot of money!

You must be saying, "Well, it's time to find another supplier." You'd be right – except that there are only three manufacturers of these products in the world and you already source from all three. Even if you could find another supplier hidden away in the back of beyond, who's to say they would be any better? It's time to grow up, break the rules, change the way the game is played, and stop losing money.

It appears that this industry does the same thing over and over again. You have to do something different, if you're going to make more money: that means reducing the costs associated with dealing with these suppliers.

You need to change the game and this is what you could do. Carefully assess all the problems that your supplier causes you and go to see them. Be constructive, not destructive, here, despite what your emotions are probably telling you! Remember how you felt when a customer told you about a problem that you didn't know about. Your supplier might not even know that all these bad moments of truth are a problem to you. How would they, unless you've told them? So tell them and work with them to iron out each problem – one at a time. For every problem you resolve with your supplier, you'll be saving money, time, and of course that huge emotional drain, frustration.

If you have a clear view of all of the interactions (customers and suppliers) with your company, then you can review precisely what happens at each interaction.

- ⤴ Get your customer services team together and explain that you want to review how you deal with customers, at each and every contact point. You want to make it a good experience. You want your customers to feel good, so that they remain as customers and buy more from you. Be clear about what you want to achieve during the session.
- ⤴ Uncover every type of interaction that your business has with customers.
- ⤴ When you've identified them all, put them in the order they happen. For example:

1 a visit to your website
2 an incoming phone enquiry or incoming email
3 the customer asks questions before they decide to buy
4 a new customer asks for a credit account
5 an order is placed
6 the order dispatched
7 the customer receives the product
8 the customer uses the product
9 something goes wrong

➲ Now work through each interaction until you have maximised the positive impact at every point.

Let's take an incoming phone call as an example.

Your customer team works from 9 am to 5:30 pm Monday to Friday. But what if your customer telephones at 8:35 am? Does that call go to an answer phone explaining that the office opens at 9 am? Are they offered the opportunity to leave a message, to call back when the office is open, or to send an e-mail, and if the latter, to whom?

As you establish what does or doesn't happen, you can overlay your brand manifesto and service standards, to help you to determine what should happen and how. A Grown-Up Business will take this opportunity to either write a new process or review an existing "broken" process and then train in the staff in the new process, so the customer will receive a consistently good moment of truth. A Grown-Up Business will be looking to see how they can do it even better.

If you have a phone tracking system, you might find that you actually have lots of calls between 8 and 9 am. You might be losing business or customers, especially if one of your competitors opens at 8 am. Perhaps you should have someone start work at 8 am for a couple of weeks, to answer the calls that you're currently missing? You could record what questions are asked and how many orders are placed before 9 am. Once you have the evidence and the facts, you can review the situation from both the customer perspective and your cost base, to make a decision about extending your opening hours.

You might discover that you don't even have an answer phone message or that there's no process or accountable person who retrieves the messages from the system and responds to them. Even if you have this service, does it give the customer options to leave a message, phone back in office hours or e-mail?

Moments of truth are important check points for both customer interactions and your interactions with suppliers. Take time to assess what happens at each interaction: this will help improve the experience. A smoother, more valuable experience makes more money.

Same again?

Just because you've always done something one way doesn't mean it's the best way – the quickest, easiest, cheapest, or most effective. The way you do it might be okay; it works, it's efficient, and it gets the job done. But if it's not the quickest, easiest, cheapest, or most effective, it's not the grown-up way of doing things. Even small changes can make big differences to your profitability.

Doing the same thing over and over again eventually becomes habit-forming. Sports people, especially golfers, talk about muscle memory; practising a really good swing motion means it becomes repetitive, more accurate more of the time. As Gary Player said, "The more I practice, the better I get." But doing the wrong thing over and over again will never help you improve. It feeds a "That's okay, that'll do' mentality, not one of continuous improvement. The challenge is to find those same-again ways of doing things and decide to change or improve them.

A Grown-Up Business strives to improve all the time. It doesn't subscribe to the "If it's not broken, don't mend it" philosophy. It's continually looking for ways to improve everything. Settling for *okay* is never okay. You don't get a buzz from *okay*, but you do get a buzz from a *wow*. "We've always done it like this" is no excuse for not bothering to review the process and the outcome.

Your business motivation might be cost savings or delighting customers. Whatever the reason, a Grown-Up Business's underlying objective is to make it better, cheaper, quicker, easier, and more efficient. For example, if you have face-to-face sales meetings with your field sales team, that's expensive. A day off the road for each salesman is 5% of their monthly production time, plus travel costs to a central venue, and so on. However, if you used technology, you could have a virtual sales meeting for two months and just a quarterly meeting face-to-face. Think how much money you would save: reduced travel costs, more production, downtime cut from a day to half a day… It's better, cheaper, quicker, easier, and more efficient all round. For everything in your business, ask yourself, "What can we do better, more quickly, more cheaply, more easily, and more efficiently?"

Repeating the same mistakes takes its toll on everyone and your bank balance too. Having to deal with product quality complaints, late deliveries, or incorrect invoices wears people down and costs you money. You have to stop, learn from your mistakes, and turn them into improvements.

To start making small changes that will make big differences, you need to take a look at what's really happening in your business. A great place to start is your complaints log. (If you don't have a complaints log, start one now: it's a great investment for any business.) Review the complaints log and highlight any recurring themes. I did this recently with one of my clients.

These clients manufacture LED lighting for large offices, warehouses, and car parks, but they had a problem: customer complaints about product quality were increasing. They sourced some of their components from overseas, then assembled the elements into bespoke lighting units before they were installed. They already had a quality control team in place and their failure rate on internal product quality checks was 3%. On the face of it, a 3% fail rate is pretty good… until we discovered that 35% of all of their complaints were about poor product quality. Inadvertently, the company had allowed its clients to become the quality control department. It was time to do something different, "same again" wasn't working, but what could they do?

They reviewed all their quality-checking procedures: each one was put under the microscope. Surprisingly, the unit's manufacture was thoroughly checked to make sure it was robust, but there were no standards for testing light intensity – one of the customer's prime complaints.

They prepared a new quality-checking procedure and put new report forms in place. They created new categories of failure and each failure was recorded on the report forms. Now a robust measurement could start.

The products made on each run were coded, so they could be traced back to the team that had made them, and each batch of components used was also recorded against each product. This meant the quality team could pin-point where future problems might come from.

Next they set about developing and implementing new testing methods for light intensity. They retrained the production and quality teams and reinforced the new processes and procedures. They tested all new components delivered to the factory before they were installed into the lighting units and kept records on each supplier's performance.

When they put the new methods in place, the internal failure rate shot up, but customer complaints stabilised and then dropped. With more satisfied customers, the company had a better chance of growing their business. But they still had work to do. They knew why product quality was poor, so they had to systematically address each aspect. Not long after they started the new process, they found a new component supplier. Then they continued to correct the broken processes. On-going reporting by shift, by day, and by week became the norm. This proved to be the best way of reducing customer complaints to virtually zero. As more improvements kicked in, the internal fail rate started to reduce and the external complaints disappeared.

It's time for action.

- ⊃ Make a list of all of the complaint themes from your complaints log, with the most common ones at the top. Those are your priority.
- ⊃ Bring your team together and explain the problem. No one likes dealing with complaints, so you need them to engage with your desire to make everyone's lives, especially the clients', better.

➲ To find out why these problems keep cropping up, you could carry out an employee survey by asking them specific questions. Alternatively, team and individual brainstorming sessions are an effective method for finding out what's really happening.

As well as resolving problems that your customers have already told you about, make sure you find out about any other problems:

➲ Have a brainstorm with your team. List everything that the business could do to upset a customer. When you have a list, flip it and make sure you do the opposite.
➲ Consider mystery-shopping your business, especially if you're a service business. Get an independent person or company to do this, as they'll tell you the truth and not what they think you want to hear!
➲ Treat complaints, customer feedback, reviews, and so on, as gold dust. Use feedback forms or set up online review forums, similar to Trip Advisor. Alternatively, send a questionnaire to your customers and ask them specific questions about your product, service, and delivery. We learn much more from our mistakes, so take each mistake, learn from it, and then improve on it.
➲ Ask your best customers what frustrates them about dealing with companies such as yours. Be prepared to listen to some home truths and remember that it's a really good way to learn. However hard it is to hear criticisms, listen, consider, learn, and then improve.

You can't make more money if you don't know what's going wrong. Of course, you could wait until your customers tell you, just as my manufacturing client did, or wait until you realise that you've lost your customers. They say, "Ignorance is bliss," but in the Grown-Up Business world, you can't afford ignorance, not even for one minute. Every minute costs you money.

All change

Change happens, regardless of what we wish for, and for the most part we deal with it, even if we struggle to embrace it. In the 90s, the business mantra was "Change or die." Those that didn't embrace the changes in our society, global economies, and technology did die, or at best really struggled to survive. Those that embraced change not only survived but thrived. But the Grown-Up Businesses not only embraced change, they instigated it. They didn't wait to react to change: they forced the change and made improvements. These Grown-Up Businesses have been the biggest winners over the past 20 years. Change can be evolutionary or revolutionary and the impact of the world outside your business affects your business, for better or for worse.

If you have had your business for several years, you'll have seen lots of changes. In addition to technological, social, and cultural changes, we have the political landscape: government changes, new laws, changed laws, new and increased taxes, new incentives and schemes. The way you do business, the rise of the internet and now of mobile information, buying habits, customer reviews, and consumers' attitudes to complaints, usually via social media, have all changed. And if you're starting your business today, you might be doing that exactly because you want to step up and change the way the game is played.

You'll never have the perfect business. Grown-Up Businesses know that, but they make changes all the time, some big, others small, all designed to correct weaknesses, take advantage of strengths, use opportunities, and resist threats. They aim to make their business the very best it can be for everyone that touches it. The mantra today is "Change and improve, continually." Again, be careful here: we don't want change for change's sake. Many aspects of your business and the market in which you operate are right. The challenge is to find the parts of your business and the market that are wrong and change those. And the best place to start is the parts of your business that immediately affect your customers.

As well as making internal changes, you must also be very aware of what's happening in the outside world, with your industry, your customers, your suppliers, the government, world events, and our society. Events in the wider world could force change on you. That can be a real problem or a fantastic opportunity for your business.

Consider the current rage against plastic carrier bags. As a plastic bag manufacturer, it's a big problem. Your market could be destroyed by changes in society and by government's enforced changes. You need a new product line and quickly. As we've seen, supermarkets have jumped on the campaign. After all, it's going to save them millions of pounds if we don't use their free carrier bags anymore. If the government introduces a mandatory charging structure, then supermarkets will need a new system to account for this money and pay taxes too. Whichever it might be, the clock has started ticking…

There's a new business world. You can capitalise on the changes and identify opportunities that weren't previously available. Who would've invented i-gloves without touchscreen phones? At least now we can have warm hands and use the phone at the same time! Are you going to react to enforced change or are you going to be proactive and drive change forward? "Change is the law of life. And those who look only to the past or the present are certain to miss the future," said John F Kennedy.

Change can be scary and uncomfortable. 20 years ago, change at the speed we're now used to was rare. 20 years ago, you could still have a job for life. Now people tend to change jobs every three to four years. The younger generation (Gen Y) are much more adaptable and receptive to change, always ready to try something new. Many of the older generation still struggle with the concept of change. But even my 81-year-old mum has an iPad and does online banking as well as online shopping!

Some change can be evolutionary: small steps, tweaks, and adjustments that happen every day. Your team will hardly notice small incremental changes, so they happen easily. Evolutionary change is very similar to the principle of continuous improvement.

Revolutionary change is another matter. It's like hurling a grenade into your business. The result is explosive and affects everything in its reach. This is not for the faint-hearted, but if it's a strategy you decide to adopt, be ready for collateral damage, casualties (probably not the ones you expected), to finish what you started. In *The Fifth Discipline*, Peter Senge quoted a seasoned change consultant as saying, "People don't resist change; they resist being changed."

Jack and Alan spotted a business opportunity as a result of changes over the past decade. They saw exactly how they could capitalise on new technology, new ways of shopping, and a reluctance of the existing players in the market to change. This, coupled with the rise of craft and the "make do and mend" trend, meant the stars were aligned for a successful launch.

Jack and Alan sell knitting wool online. They have no physical shops on the high street. They offer free postage and packaging on all orders over £15 and if you order before 3 pm, you get next-day delivery. The website is clear and uncluttered; the shopping basket is a great experience. They've introduced an up-to-the-minute stock system and only products that are in stock are advertised for sale. You can shop by colour, ply, price range, or brand.

They built followers, customers, and advocates via social media and pay-per-click, but it was the word-of-mouth referrals and online feedback that really rocketed sales. Why? They did exactly what they said they would do for the customers. They focused on making buying wool a great experience for the customer every time. They embraced the change that was happening in the wider world. As a result, they revolutionised the market for knitting wool sales.

On the basis that not everything in your business is perfect, you need to consider what has to be changed. At this early stage, you should only be looking for evolutionary or incremental change internally. The problem is that revolutionary change from the wider world might be looming on the horizon – you need to be prepared!

Lift your head away from your desk and take a look at the wider world. What's happening in the external world that could impact on your business in either a negative or positive way?

- ➲ Think about the social, legal, environmental, economic, political and technology changes that are happening around you. Make a list under each of the headings of things that you need to consider.
- ➲ Now ask yourself, what is the biggest opportunity and the biggest threat to your business? How soon or how likely are they to happen? What might be the impact on your company?
- ➲ On a less revolutionary note, what can you learn from other industries and markets – how do they run their businesses? What could you implement from another industry in your business that would make a big difference?

KISS principle

The more complex a task, process, or system is, the more chance something will go wrong. If a product is complicated or over engineered, it's more expensive to produce. The more moving parts or functionality that you include, the more susceptible a product is to break down or malfunction.

Adding more options and extras to your services adds a great deal of complexity to your sales messages, pricing plans, and execution. If it's too complicated, the customer won't be able to understand what they're going to get and so they won't buy!

complexity = more cost + increased risks

The KISS principle is "Keep It Simple, Stupid!" If you simplify the functions in your business, you can make even more money. Grown-Up Businesses are very good at keeping things simple. I don't like the "stupid" bit of the phrase, but if someone doesn't focus on simplifying all their business, then the stupid hat will have to fit. Why would anyone make the whole shebang so complicated and expensive, when a cheaper, easier, quicker version can be just as good?

Error rates, mistakes, and omissions increase with complexity and boy do they add cost to your bottom line – costs that you must eliminate if you're going to make more money.

Every aspect of your business can be simplified, from your sales process through to accounts, production, packaging, dispatch, marketing, and pricing. Just think of the plethora of energy or mobile phone tariffs to see how complex a company can become. This type of complexity can confuse customers to the point where they don't buy at all. Simplifying your business makes it easier for customers to do business with you.

Let's consider your marketing efforts. In the good old days before social media marketing erupted onto the scene, you could employ many marketing activities: direct mail, exhibitions, printed brochures, press, face-to-face sales, telemarketing, and advertising of all types. That was complicated enough: trying to get the best mix of the marketing elements was challenging. Now we also have social media and online marketing to contend with: Facebook, LinkedIn, Twitter, YouTube, Instagram, Google+, websites, email campaigns, blogs, banners, comments, webinars, video, podcasts… and I'm sure a few more will be along soon! Wow, complex or what? Each different element adds to your profile, your visibility, your client and prospect engagement, and your brand positioning, but it also adds cost and complexity to your business. The cost isn't necessarily hard cash – it might be extra staff, more resources, or more software systems to help you.

It's easy to see how marketing can get a bad reputation for wasting money and why so many companies outsource to specialists. If you tried to execute every element of the marketing mix, you'd be overwhelmed with work, costs and people. Time to take stock and simplify your approach.

A start-up company approached me for help. They'd developed a new product: a bobbin with a cover and winder to keep cables on chargers under control. They'd become frustrated with all their chargers and cables getting tangled up like spaghetti. A great invention for neat freaks. The product looked great and did what it said on the tin. However, the initial design had so many components and functions that the cost to make it was putting it out of the market's reach. They planned to offer multiple colours and sizes, again adding to the range's complexity as well as to the manufacturing process.

Back to the drawing board they went. They reviewed colour first and decided on just black and white – the only colours of cable chargers. Problem simplified. Size was next. They decided to move to a one-size-fits-all approach by making sure that the longest cable available on any charger would fit within the bobbin. Problem simplified.

Finally, functionality. In their research, they discovered that in 95% of cases, the charger stays in the same place once it's plugged in. They decided to remove the winding handle because customers could easily wind the cable into the bobbin by hand, especially as they didn't need to do so often. Problem simplified.

It's easy to slip into complexity. I've fallen into the trap of designing the "perfect" workshop, packed to overflowing with content, a huge slide pack, a printed workbook for every delegate… But that came at a cost to me: time to write all the elements, to print paper packs, to design slides and workbooks for the workshop every time, and then I was asked to send e-versions too. Add to that the high overheads at the hotel for room and food for a full-day workshop.

It turned out the clients didn't want a full day or all the paper. In trying to deliver the ultimate workshop, I'd added unnecessary expense that they didn't value. The result was a poorly attended and unprofitable exercise for my business. So I KISSed it. Now it's shorter, less complicated, and cheaper for me. More people attend, so I make more money overall and I'm far less stressed too.

Your business will have developed complexity over time and if you haven't kept that in check, it will be wasting time, money and resources. Take the process map from chapter 5 and critically review one process.

- ➲ Look for anything you can simplify. Can you shorten forms, so they're quicker to complete and easier to key into the computer? Can you go further and get rid of the paper all together, to avoid any typing or keying errors? Maybe scan the form or have it completed on computer.
- ➲ Now look at a product or service that you deliver. Look at all the elements, one by one. How could you make the product or service simpler and therefore cheaper for you to supply? Remember that the product must still do what it says on the tin. You might just need to find a cheaper component or material, or a training venue where the coffee is a reasonable price!
- ➲ As an ongoing exercise when you're doing any task, take a few moments to review it and ask yourself, "Is there an easier way?" Which elements are essential and which are nice but expensive? If you were a stranger or an alien coming into your company, what would you do to simplify it?

The KISS philosophy must pervade your entire business, so that you avoid unnecessary complexity and focus on the simplest, most effective solution.

Remove the waste

Like many women, I love to shop, updating my wardrobe with everything from clothes to shoes, bags, and accessories. I buy something new, then

I fail miserably to get rid of an old item from my wardrobe. Do I really need a new storage cupboard for all those handbags that I no longer use? At some point, it all gets too much and I have a massive cull, giving items to friends and charity, sending bits to the rubbish tip or recycling, maybe even reselling on eBay.

We've established that you can make more money by reducing complexity. Now we're going to consider what you can remove from your business altogether. Simplifying your business is all about replacing, reducing, and removing cost and complexity. Our focus now shifts to removals.

In striving to become a Grown-Up Business, companies soon realise that they need to have a clear-out: remove the clutter and find the parts of their business that are overburdened or stifled by excessive work, streamline resources and systems. In most businesses, this decluttering is triggered by a fall in profits and income or a rise in overheads and expenses. To cut costs, you need to remove waste in your business. Every business, without exception, has wasted resources, be they time, money, people or effort.

With increased awareness of the environment, waste in this area has been (or should have been) tackled already. We all see the benefits and cost savings of being an environmentally conscious organisation. Simple things like turning out lights or turning the heating down when it's not needed make a big difference to your costs. So in the same way that you'd conduct an energy audit on your business, audit your business for waste in the remaining areas. While rose-tinted spectacles distort the real world into a rosy one, a pair of waste-seeking spectacles will focus your attention on seeking out the waste in your company. Everywhere you look, waste is around you and it's costing you money! Concentrate on four main areas: wasted money, time, effort and resources.

Money

- What unnecessary purchases are you making?
- When was the last time you looked to see if you could buy an item better?
- How many subscriptions do you pay monthly that you don't need any more? It's so easy to set up a direct debit mandate and so easy to ignore those £10 sums going out each month.

- Review what you're spending, especially those direct debits.
- Do you have a purchase order system? Who in your company can spend what, without your knowledge? Review your purchase order system to make sure it's effective or, if you don't have one, set one up.
- Who checks the payment runs before they're made?
- How much "dead stock" do you have that just isn't selling? It's tying up cash, so you can't reinvest. The cost of dead money can cripple a business.

Time

In your business, time is money. If something wastes time, it costs money. Delays cost money. Working on completely the wrong tasks costs money. Continuing to work on a project that isn't going to work costs money. Employing underperforming staff costs money. Doing something twice costs money.

Effort

Double-handling means unloading stock to one place and then having to go back to move it into its final resting place – it's a waste of effort. In the same way, if we waste time on the wrong tasks or have to do something again, the effort we put in is wasted too. This makes it doubly important to remove the waste.

Resources

People are probably the biggest cost. If you have the wrong people or too many people, then money is seeping out of your business. Sadly, it's human nature for employees to keep doing the same work even if it's been replaced by new systems.

Preparing management information is a classic example. As time passes, the business owner needs new or amended reports on the business. Maybe they were prepared by a person in the past, but now you can press a button and see your digital dashboard on your screen. How many reports are prepared that have been superseded and no one looks at anymore, but a person in your company still prepares them? Remove the waste and you'll find your team has more capacity to achieve more important things.

Ultimately, you might even be able to save a head count, their salary, and all of the associated costs.

The Recruitment Co Ltd has been trading for over 20 years. Business was good – plenty of cash in the bank, no debt. They didn't need to think about spending money anymore: they had it so they could spend it. Controls slipped, process and procedures were ignored, and cheques were just signed.

Then everything changed. It was a combination of events – big bad debt, losing a key sales person, a director's illness – and suddenly the cash cushion was gone. Debt started to increase. They had to make savings, so they did the obvious. They cut staff, cancelled those long-forgotten subscriptions, changed to cheaper suppliers, and reduced overheads. But they'd missed one. The boss opened her desk drawer one Friday afternoon for some more staples and found not one but four boxes in her drawer – enough to last her a full year. She looked closer: six pads of Post-it notes, numerous pens and pencils, all sorts of paraphernalia. She cleared her desk drawers, amazed at the amount of stationery hidden in them. She did some quick mental maths on how much had it all cost. Then she looked at the other 15 desks in the office. It gave her quite a jolt.

When everyone had gone home that night, she relieved every desk drawer of its entire office supplies – what a pile. Next, she left one of each item on top of the desk ready for Monday morning. Now to refill the stationery cabinet. It overflowed with supplies and the business didn't buy a single stationery item for the next 12 months. The Recruitment Company Ltd had been spending £100 a month and it took one member of staff the equivalent of one day a month to collect everyone's requests, prepare the order, find the best supplier, deal with the delivery when it arrived, and account for and pay the invoice.

She reinstated the purchasing process controls and then reminded the entire team that they were a Grown-Up Business. They had to exercise controls and ask questions before any action, let alone spending money. She saved money and time.

Waste can creep up on you and overwhelm the company without you even noticing. You need to do something different: it needs your attention *now* if you're going to become a Grown-Up Business and make more money.

➲ Draw down a full list of all of your outgoings from the past month.
➲ Review each one and decide…

1 Do you still need it (such as subscriptions and regular payments)?
2 When did you last review the prices you're paying? Is there a cheaper, better supplier?
3 Do you know what the spend was for? Who in your company is buying this and why?
4 What costs can you pass onto your customers? For example, if a customer requests a special courier delivery, do you absorb that cost or charge it to the customer?

Plug the gaps

Now that you've removed complexity, duplication, and waste, you need to make sure that you plug any gaps. A gap in a process or system can lose you both time and money. For example, you might meet a new prospect, say at an exhibition or conference, and conclude the meeting with "I'll call you next week" or "I'll send you our proposal." It doesn't happen, though, because you didn't capture their details from the business card before you lost it. That's not only a big mistake, it's a gap that must be plugged in the future. It's hard enough to secure new clients and keep existing ones, but if you let them fall through the cracks in the floorboards, that costs you money in terms of a lost opportunity. The processes you developed in chapter 5 are your starting point. Seek out the gaps, find the cracks between the floorboards, and plug them.

In most cases, gaps occur in sales, marketing, and customer services departments. Production, service delivery, and accounts tend to be more process orientated, so they generally suffer less from the problem of gaps. That's not to say that there aren't any, but your first priority is to review sales, marketing and customer services.

With the explosion of automated processes such as telephone systems, auto-enrolments, online purchasing, and so on, a Grown-Up Business's best practice is to regularly test them and eliminate any gremlins that might have crept in. For example, if you've used an 0845 number on a series of adverts, you need to check that phone number still works and who's actually going to answer that call, before you use it again. Trust me – it's worth checking.

I recently worked with a main car dealership team who were concerned about falling sales and the lack of responses to their promotions from off-the-page advertising. We discovered that they had a subscription for 43 0845 numbers. They'd been set up to track the impact of off-the-page advertisements for a number of different local newspapers, as well as for each of the three car marques that the dealership sold. We also uncovered the performance report from the 0845 telephone number supplier. Several of the numbers had only recorded unanswered calls. Time for some investigating. We called every one of the numbers and found…

- 7 weren't connected
- 9 went to the wrong branch
- 4 had messages saying they were on holiday with no forwarding number
- 6 went to the wrong car marque

26 of the 43 numbers were virtually useless. On the 7 unconnected lines, there were a total of 326 unanswered calls. Even if you assume that each person dialled twice, thinking they'd misdialled the first time, then that's 160 missed opportunities. Did they visit the dealership? (At least the address on the advert was correct.) Maybe. Did they go to another garage dealership? Possibly. Did they moan about the company to others? Probably.

All the 0845 numbers were reviewed, deleted, or directed to the right person. Every time they placed an advert, one of the team called the 0845 number to check it worked and who answered it.

By plugging the gaps in telephone answering, all their calls got through to the right person. The next quarter, sales were back on track.

The same applies to email sign-ups for a newsletter or free download. Someone gives their e-mail and contact details and the website tells them they'll get an e-mail with a link to the download. Does it arrive? Does it work? If they can't access the download, how will they be able to read the content or see the call to action that you've put in? They'll just fall into a black hole and you've lost them as a potential customer.

Focus on one process that interacts with a customer. If you have a 0845 number system or an email sign-up, why not start there?

- ⮑ Put your actual process under the microscope and really study what happens at each and every interaction.
- ⮑ Ask yourself what could go *wrong* at each interaction, rather than what *should* happen. Once you know what could go wrong, you can test to see whether that's happening or not and then correct it.
- ⮑ Make sure that you test your own automated systems regularly. You should also be checking your email addresses from your website. Email accounts such as info@, sales@, admin@, and so on, need to be allocated to a specific person and the emails need to be dealt with.

Outsource

As you grow your business, the natural progression is to do more inside the company: employ more staff to help you, take on bigger premises, invest in more stock, and develop more products and services. Sometimes it feels like you're feeding an insatiable giant. The more it grows, the more money it needs, and of course that's true. Any growing business will burn cash. But you don't have to follow convention: you can do something different and make more money.

Grown-Up Businesses are also great outsourcers. To them, outsourcing is a cost-effective, cost-saving strategy. Advantages of outsourcing include…

- you get the best experts for any specialised work
- you save costs – it's generally cheaper than paying a full-time person
- you save time in set-up costs, recruitment, etc
- you reduce errors and mistakes
- you can flex your capacity up or down
- you improve your capability

Typical outsourced services include virtual assistants, call answering, bookkeeping, marketing, PR, online services, building maintenance, logistics, stock-taking, purchasing, catering, training, security, legal services, accountancy, banking services, insurance broking, and so on. You can also add the substantial outsourcing of manufacturing to China, the mushrooming of call centres in India, and the online capabilities in Eastern Europe of which UK companies take advantage.

Outsourcing has impacted practically every business and virtually all companies outsource something. Even companies that specialise in providing outsourcing services also outsource themselves.

In a micro-business, you'd outsource your bookkeeping, VAT, and annual accounting. As you grow, you then outsource to a management accountant for a day or two a month, increasing the days as the business demands more high-level financial support. Employing a full-time financial controller from day one would be very expensive and they'd be twiddling their thumbs for most of the week.

Outsourcing has its downsides, primarily because many business owners abdicate responsibility. They tend to think that it's "off my desk", so they don't need to manage it, but in actual fact they do.

When setting up outsourcing arrangements, there are some golden rules:

- Create a robust service-level agreement (SLA). This sets out what has to be done, to what standard, by when, and for whom. It may also include penalties for non-compliance.
- Choose your provider carefully. With call centres and manufacturing outsourced to India and China, it's a long way to travel if something goes wrong and you need a face-to-face discussion. Personally, I prefer any outsourcing services to be within a maximum of a two-hour drive. That way, if necessary, I can drive to see them and talk face-to-face to resolve any issues.
- Set your culture and standards. If you're the Rolls-Royce standard in your industry, you'll need Rolls-Royce outsourcers. They must have the same ethos and care as you do. Their standards must be at least equivalent to yours.
- Don't abdicate – ever!

I include freelancers, interim managers and directors, and temporary staff in this category. Part of a director's role is to build good teams for both day-to-day and project work. Just as you would pull a project team together, you need to use outsourcers of all types to make up your team members.

If you're the sole owner and manager of your business, you need a team and the best way to get one is to hire really good experts via the outsourcing model: your accountant, your bank manager, your PR, your coach, your lawyer, and your insurance broker. Tap into their expertise without having to pay their full-time salaries.

The Car Cleaning Co Ltd is an online trading company that sources and resells car-cleaning products. Until I started work with them, I never knew car cleaning was such an art – a bucket, sponge, soap and a hosepipe does me very well! They sell the products of the "five-hour car clean" and that's just the outside. But the results are fantastic and the products' consumers are fanatical.

The Car Cleaning Co Ltd has three members of staff: the boss and two support staff, who work in a three-desk office. That's it. They could've had every aspect of the business run and staffed in-house, but instead they followed an outsourcing model. Everything except the online marketing and customer services is outsourced.

All their products are kept in a pick-and-pack warehouse. The outsourced pick-and-pack company manage stock levels, reorder levels, customer orders, packaging, despatch, and reporting. The Car Cleaning Co Ltd doesn't need to buy or rent large premises, buy a forklift truck, or hire a warehouseman, a packer, a dispatcher, a recorder, or a reporter. Everything is handled by the outsourced company, for a fee of course. The numbers add up for The Car Cleaning Co Ltd. It costs much less to outsource all these services than to have them in-house. Another advantage is that in peak selling times, they don't have to find extra staff to handle the extra order level – the outsourcers handle that too.

To outsource, you have to start to let go.

➲ Take one job or task in your company that you dislike doing, is a cheaper job to do, or you can't do, and decide to let it go to someone outside your business.

➲ Find two or three organisations supplying the outsourcing service you need.

➲ Write a brief (similar to a job description, but for a company) and include what has to be done, when, to what standard, and with what results.

➲ Check out the outsourcers, just as you would if you were employing a person, and interview them. When they mirror your brand and service standards, and understand your business, then engage them to deliver your service requirements.

➲ The time and money you've saved can now be used for the important parts of growing your business.

Doing something different will make you more money. To start with, you need to focus on small parts of your business, not all of it, and you'll see improvements straight away. Whether it's implementing change, shedding complexity, removing waste, plugging the gaps, or outsourcing, you'll be a more Grown-Up Business.

Chapter 7

Reaching Maturity

As we've seen, growing up is full of challenges. If you meet the challenges head on with a plan and focus, success can be sweet. Just because you've achieved success, though, doesn't mean your future success is guaranteed. Far from it. Complacency is the downfall of many. Assuming everything is under control is dangerous. In many respects, the hard work starts again here.

In this chapter we walk through streamlining the business and really start to scale up. Order, systems, and processes are critical to scaling up the business and expecting the unexpected. My Six-Step Process to Brilliant Processes will guide you step by step through listing, mapping, measuring, improving, documenting, and training.

Systematise to scale up

The only way to become a bigger, more successful business is to scale up. Dragon and angel investors are always looking for scalability; it's the number one item on their checklist. But you have no chance of scaling up a business if everything is kept in your head. You absolutely have to systematise your business.

First we need to understand why many businesses just can't seem to grow. They try to grow, it spirals out of control or fails miserably, and they give up and then focus on becoming a small business again!

New problems arise as you grow, but the old ones keep reappearing, draining your resources, and you just end up firefighting all the time. Waste mushrooms, in the form of money, people and time. Your margins erode as your costs rise more quickly than your turnover. Your cash reserves are stretched; cash flow is under pressure. You employ more expensive people to get things done. You continue to work harder in the business, but not on the business. Consistency evades you in every area: service to customers, product quality, delivery and performance, employees, suppliers. Because you try to do everything, you become the business. It's totally reliant on you. All in all, it's a chaotic mess: far too many plates spinning with too many stressed people wasting even more time and money.

But growing a business can be done. Just look at that single burger joint in the USA that now has a bigger economy than Ecuador: McDonald's, the most successful small business to scale ever. It's located in over 115 countries and still expanding with many more restaurants being opened worldwide, and 58 million customers are served each day with identical products and service. It's the world's largest distributor of toys. It has increased shareholder dividends every year for 25 years.

So, what did Ray Kroc do differently? He standardised an entire system for successfully running a business. He re-engineered every process to maximise profit. He insisted on consistency – that the five-thousandth burger should be as good as the first. He made the business systems-dependent, not person-dependent. He left a business model that didn't fail when the boss left. He relentlessly focused his time on working on the business, not in it.

The rules of a scalable business are…

- consistent value to the customer, employees, and suppliers
- business operated by people with the lowest possible level of skill
- stands out as a place of impeccable order
- every process, system or procedure is documented, then refined and improved over and over again
- uniformly predictable service to the customer
- the boss is dispensable

If you want to work a few hours a week and ensure that your customers receive the same product, whether it's the first or five-thousandth, then you have to develop a failure proof standard approach that is a replicable, profit-maximising series of processes. Once you have this in place, (plus your dream team, rules and boundaries) then and only then can you think about a full or partial exit of the business, or perhaps even a franchise model!

Paul runs a training company that specialises in residential training courses and accreditation. He has grown his business very well and also trains some of our ex-servicemen who are returning to civvy street.

His business was at bursting point, because he didn't have the back-office systems in place to handle any more courses. However, they were starting to build a second residential block which would double their capacity – if only they could fill it without the back office cracking under the pressure.

The business was run entirely on spreadsheets, Outlook diaries, and contacts. It was a great system for a small business, but Paul's company had outgrown these systems and his growth was severely hampered. They were in danger of the whole thing imploding.

For Paul to scale up, he had to systematise the business. The big leap forward was to understand which parts of each process could be automated. The answer was a lot. He set about flowcharting the systems and processes with his team and then worked to improve them. An introduction from me to a systems company was the big turning point for his business. An off-the-shelf system was ready and waiting, needing only a little customisation. As a result, over 50% of the manual systems were automated.

The team took three months to get the new systems in place, then the marketing campaign kicked off. With the new systems in place, they were able to ensure that the new residential unit was fully occupied from day one.

How can you systematise the business so that it can be replicated 5,000 times and the last one runs as smoothly as the first? How would you demonstrate and prove the business model to a buyer or franchisee? After all, the franchisee is buying a business in a box. How can you own and still control the business but be free of it? How can you quadruple the value of your business in just a few weeks? How can you have very happy repeat-purchasing customers, a dream team of employees and suppliers so eager to supply you that you can drive a better deal? The answer to all of these is to create a business that is orderly and run with processes.

A place for everything and everything in its place

There's nothing more annoying than starting a DIY job and finding something missing. You were raring to go; now you're stopped in your tracks. Do you waste the time you'd set aside on a trip back to the shops or stop the job and do something else? Frustrating as it may be in our private lives, it's even more maddening at work. Imagine a production line coming to a halt because one component isn't where it should be when it's needed. Even a temporary shutdown will be expensive. Imagine trying to track a customer order in a warehouse full of orders, finding you don't have it, incurring the extra cost of ordering more stock, only to find you already have a stockpile of that order stored in the wrong warehouse! Imagine searching for the first-aid kit to treat an injured worker – and what the consequences could be.

In a Grown-Up Business, everything is in its right place at the right time. It's orderly, tidy, clean, and safe. Desks are clear, workshops clean and well organised, vehicles and plants are fully maintained, stock and materials are ready to be used or sold, tools and spares are all present and correct, files are in the right order so you can find what you're looking for quickly.

Everything runs smoothly, as if by magic. The "magic" is that the entire business has been organised around its systems, processes, and procedures, making sure there are no inefficiencies. That way, the customer gets the same quality of service or product every time. No inconsistencies, ever. Being super-efficient while maintaining a consistent customer experience is how Grown-Up Businesses make more money.

Employees, just like all humans, are consistently inconsistent when left to their own devices. One person has a completely different way of doing the same task to another. One may order materials when there's ten days' stock left; another when there are three days to go. And what happens if both are away and someone else is in charge? No warning flag, so nothing is ordered.

We're human: we make mistakes, forget something, or just ignore it. By setting up your operating framework so it doesn't rely on human memory, you can maximise productivity, ensure consistency, and enhance the customer's experience all at once. Business life will get easier when everyone knows where everything is, how the business operates, and why everything should be in its place.

Denise runs two restaurants with a third about to open. The menus are the same at each restaurant, but some dishes are more popular in one restaurant than the other. She wants customers to always have the entire menu to choose from, so she has to pay particular attention to her food orders. She also needs enough clean linen, plates, glasses, wine, chocolate, and coffee.

When Denise made the move from one restaurant to two, she soon realised that she had to get more organised. She found it hard to remember which restaurant she'd placed an order for. One restaurant had too much food and the other not enough. Food was spoiling and had to be thrown away. Some tables ran out of clean tablecloths and customers soon realised standards were dropping. Something had to change. She had to put in systems and standardisation if she was to avoid all that wastage and chaos. The first thing to do was to make sure that everything had a place.

Today, her restaurants have clear processes to make sure that both front of house and the kitchen have what they need when they need it. All products are stored in the same place every time. The kitchen store is a neat freak's paradise: each shelf is labelled, with new products put to the back of the shelf when they arrive. Orders are crosschecked against the delivery notes and taken to their final spot straight away – no delay, no boxes for staff to fall over, no frozen food defrosting all over the floor. Because the delivery's only moved once, straight into the correct place, stock check and reordering are easier and more accurate: there's only one place to look.

- ⊃ Take a walk around your premises when everyone's gone home. How tidy is it? Does it look as though your team has abandoned ship or is everything in its place? Where do you need to tidy up, organise your systems and processes, plan your storage, and straighten up your workplace?
- ⊃ If your premises are chaotic and untidy, what health and safety issues are lurking? Tidy up and avoid slips, trips, and falls now.
- ⊃ Take another walk around when the business is in full swing. What do you see that needs changing? How are your staff working? Are they stressed or calm? Are their work areas organised or messy?
- ⊃ Does what you see meet your standards? If not, where's the failure and what do you need to do to correct it?

The six steps to writing brilliant processes

As Sam Carpenter says, "There needs to be a process to define a process. And a process to refine and improve a process too!" This model shows the process, with a detailed explanation of each step below.

The six steps to writing brilliant processes

1. List your key business processes

Anything that has to be repeated must have a process. In the end, everything should have a process – even how to open the shop in the morning and make the tea! Make sure you sort out customer systems first. Much of that should already be in place, from exploring your moments of truth in chapter 6. Then look at internal systems, supplier systems, and management systems.

Some typical business processes are…

- **sales**: process, payments, order tracking, delivery, returns, refunds, complaints, performance, commission payments…
- **finance**: money in and out, credit limits, credit control, overtime authorisation, paying suppliers, bills, procurement, wages…

- **health & safety**: risk assessment, waste management, facilities, accidents...
- **IT**: file structures, archiving, content, format, templates...
- **people**: recruitment, disciplinary procedures, reward, training, holidays...
- **manufacturing**: materials, storage, stock control, processing times, recipes, order of work, breakdowns, planned maintenance...
- **marketing**: social media, copy sign off, brochure production, pricing, discounting, lead tracking, CRM...

What next?

Finalise the list of your processes and prioritise them – customer impact ones first, money second, and so on.

2. Map the process

Ingredients

- Post-it notes
- pens – lots of colours
- Blu-tack
- flip chart, roll of wallpaper, white board or a blank wall
- your team, present and motivated

Method

State the process you're mapping. Remember, you're mapping it as it is now. Put each task, however small, on one Post-it note and pop it up on the wall in a rough order. Each team member must contribute to this part. As a team, shuffle the Post-it notes into the right order. As the boss, try to facilitate this part rather than do it yourself.

Take a break, then ask yourself:

- Does the flowchart truly represent the day-to-day reality in both tasks and sequence?
- Have you really mapped it as it is, not how it should be?
- Have the team members contributed all of their knowledge?
- What improvement objectives are you setting?
  - o saving money / people / resources
  - o strengthening the process

o   eliminating waste

o   improving the experience for whoever it might be

Now you'll need to make a note (on another Post-it – a different colour perhaps) of any files, systems, or other processes that need to be accessed to complete this task – for example, the purchase ledger file.

3. Measure the process

What management information do you have to demonstrate what's happening in the process? For example, if you have a 0845 number, your supplier will give you minute-by-minute performance figures. You might see that dropped calls double between 12 and 1 pm or that 10% of your calls are received after 5 pm but you don't have an answer phone – or you do have an answer phone but who picks up the messages the next day? As always what gets measured gets done, so are you measuring the right things?

You'll need to…

- decide what measures you want in place to track effectiveness and / or efficiency
- add measurement points to the flowchart
- interpret the numbers by asking, "What is the data telling us?"

4. Improve the process

Now that you have the process as is and your objectives alongside, you can start to improve the process. Your key tasks here are to understand where the problems are, what their root causes are, and how to strip out any waste.

Find the problems

The next challenge with your team is to identify and flag any gaps, holes, dead ends, duplicated, or outdated work in the process. A gap would be the answer-phone not being checked first thing in the morning. A hole would the 12–1 pm slot for phone answering. Duplicated work might be sending a phone message to two people, just in case. Outdated work would be a handwritten note rather than voicemail or email phone message. A dead end could be taking a message and not delivering it to anyone!

Strip out the waste

If I were to visit your business and put my "waste goggles" on, what sort of things would I see happening (or not happening) that would be a "waste" or not adding value? Think about...

- unnecessary delays or duplications within the process
- wasted effort – activities that don't return enough value, possibly a "sledgehammer to crack a nut" or simple duplication
- unnecessary movements – excessive travel, poor factory layout, too much walking, stock moves too many times...
- unclear communication – wasted time having to redo something or taking time seeking clarification when messages or instructions are unclear
- incorrect inventory – activities as a result of something (or someone) not being available or having too much resource or stock "just in case"
- opportunity lost – to gain, retain, or win something
- errors – cost of rectifying mistakes, defective products, and complaint handling

Now review your process again with your "waste goggles" on. Be a stranger; think about what's stopping the process from flowing even more smoothly. What do you see?

Time to go back to your process and make the improvements. Don't change it for change's sake: refine and improve are the key words. Rework the Post-it notes into the process that it *should* be.

A good test is to make the process as foolproof as possible. Imagine that you are writing a process for a five-year-old to bake a cake:

- reduce the ingredients to a minimum
- reduce the number of steps to a minimum
- remove as much complexity as possible
- show what the finished product should look like – a photograph, perhaps

5. Document and train

There are a number of different ways to document the process: flow charts, Word documents, Excel spreadsheets. It doesn't matter which format you use, but make it consistent across every process. Your staff will thank you for leading with consistency!

As we discussed in chapter 5, all your processes need to be centrally stored. Online is best, because when the authorised person makes a change to the process, everyone will then be working to the new process, not the old one.

Simply documenting isn't enough. It's no good having a brilliant process that no one knows about or one that they don't understand. Train your team on the process – the rigid process with no variations.

With documenting and training complete, your role now is to manage the process, using the measurement points to guide you. Every process should also be formally reviewed at a point in the future, so set a review date now and stick to it.

6. Improve

Complete the circle and start the cycle again. You want to develop, implement, and refine your processes so that the business can run profitably without you and customers get a consistent experience, every time.

The benefits of solid system of processes are multiple. It helps with risk assessments and risk analysis, with compliance, with audit trails, and with complaint handling. It saves money by removing duplication and variation, requiring fewer skilled staff, and reducing waste (time, money, people, and product). It promotes consistency and enables better planning of both capacity and resources as your business grows. It makes money through more repeat purchases and word of mouth recommendations, plus new customers are easier to attract and you can charge a higher price for your product or service. You have happier people, everywhere!

Sue and Jane provide IT support to many companies. One of their services is a helpdesk. They take lots of calls from customers whose systems have a glitch. The process is as follows:

- The client calls with details of the problem.
- The call handler records the problem and enters it into a work log which goes into a queue for the next technician to work on.
- The technician receives the query and sets about fixing it.
- Once it's solved, the client is told the solution.

It's a relatively simple process, but one that Sue and Jane were able to simplify, improve, and save money on. The main change they made was automating the process. They gave every customer a portal login so that they could log queries directly onto the system. Now the query went straight to the technician and bypassed the call handler. This stopped the problem being incorrectly interpreted. The customer was able to say exactly what was wrong.

With the new system, everything became trackable: time between the request being submitted and the technician's response, any queries raised with the client, and any correspondence through to the problem being solved. This information helped Sue and Jane further refine the process. They posted a series of FAQs on their web portal, so that clients could do some basic checks before logging a request for a technician. This saved even more time and money as clients were able to self-diagnose and get back to work more quickly, saving time for everyone.

Sue and Jane saved a whole salary because they no longer needed a call handler and the customers loved the new automated service. Anne, their call handler, was so good that she took on a new challenge and still works for Jane and Sue in a new role.

➲ Now use the Six-Step Process to Brilliant Processes to define a process with your team.

Expect the unexpected

There's always something ready to throw a spanner in the works! Sadly, far too many businesses are not prepared for the unexpected. When the spanner arrives, most just muddle through. Stress levels rise, tempers fray, customers are let down, and staff feel the pressure. That can all be avoided. One of my clients, Beate, is fond of quoting John Jay's saying, "Hope for the best plan and prepare for the worst." Even Grown-Up Businesses are hit by the unexpected, but they will have planned for many scenarios.

Imagine that your main supplier has a devastating fire at their factory and are unable to supply your materials. What would you do?

The Bishopsgate bomb on Saturday 24 April 1993 was totally unexpected. It struck at the heart of the City of London and many companies were affected. Call it British spirit, but the majority of those businesses were up and running on Monday morning, albeit from other locations: their disaster recovery plans had kicked in.

The earthquake in Japan on 11 March 2011 happened thousands of miles from our shores, but for many UK companies purchasing Japanese products, their supply line was cut overnight.

Everyone pulls together in a crisis and that's a really good thing. Your role as the boss is to get your people to pull together before the crisis happens. You need to identify possible risks and plan what you would do if that happened. It's time to put in some more processes, this time under the heading of "If x happens, we will do y."

You have a responsibility to lots of people – customers, investors, staff and the community – to think one step ahead, identifying threats while they're still in the distance. By understanding the possible risks, their probability, and the impact that they'll have on your company, you can put processes in place to overcome them. It's not only events beyond your control that you should be planning for; your growth will change the business too, so you'll need to update your processes to avoid getting caught out!

Once you've identified the risks and assessed their probability, you can start to mitigate them. Alongside your mitigation strategy, you should also design processes that kick in when a particular event happens.

Forward thinking and planning will make sure that you keep providing a consistent customer experience throughout the problem period, however long that may last. Risk assessment, audits, and ongoing risk management are a top priority for you. This is so important that many companies have a risk-management committee within the board. If you ignore risk management and planning for the unexpected, your business is vulnerable.

As the business grows, it becomes more complex and this complexity leads to increased and multifaceted risks. The Grown-Up Business way of managing that is to expect the unexpected.

Terry owns a plumbing supplies company and his business is growing fast. He was planning to move to larger premises when I visited him one day. One of my other clients had moved premises recently and the phone company had let them down. Six weeks without a phone line had caused chaos and cost the business a lot of money.

I relayed the story and Terry put plans in place, just in case the phone company let him down too. He called them right away and they assured him that the switchover was booked in and all would be well – but it wasn't. On the day, they let him down with a big bump.

Fortunately, the impact on his business was slight and customers didn't notice any drop in service. Why? He'd planned for the worst. He diverted his landlines to mobiles and arranged alternate internet facilities. He also wrote to his customers and suppliers telling them he was moving and explaining that should they have any trouble contacting him, here were three different ways they could get in touch.

A little forward thinking and planning saved a whole pile of stress and lost custom.

Find somewhere quiet, sit down with pen and paper in hand, and let's start.

⊃ Jot down all the things you can think of that might be classed as unexpected. Along with the normal "factory burns down" risks, here are 10 business risks that you might not have thought of:

1 A key member of staff or even a syndicate of most or all of your employees wins the lottery.
2 You forget to renew your domain name and someone else buys it.
3 Your telephone company digs up the phone and broadband lines.
4 Your supplier's factory floods so you can't get stock.
5 Your accountant forgets to file your year-end accounts.
6 You are overwhelmed with new business.
7 Several clients go bust owing you money in the same month.
8 You are hacked.
9 Birds or bats nest in a crucial place in the premises.
10 Commodities prices or exchange rates move against you.

⊃ Put the list to one side and go for a walk. When you get back, you'll be able to add more things to your list. Your subconscious brain will have been working while you were walking!

⊃ Shuffle the list so that the most probable risk is at the top: this is the one you start with.

⊃ Write down what you would do if that event happened.

⊃ List out which processes need to be adapted and where you need to design and write the new process.

Running this exercise as a team works particularly well, as you'll get different views and solutions to consider. However, traditional group brainstorming, where everyone comes up with ideas together, is now being overtaken by a two-stage process. First, individuals work on their own to come up with ideas; next, then combine the group's ideas to select the best. (For more on this process and the research behind it, you can read "Building on the ideas of others: An examination of the idea combination process" by Kohn, Paulus, and Choi, in *Journal of Experimental Social Psychology* 2011.)

The reality is that when you run a business, improvement work never stops. Complacency cannot be allowed to creep in. Tracking performance against your processes will be critical. You have to know what is working and what isn't, then you can make improvements.

Opinions are divided on companies such as Amazon and McDonald's – in fact, on most big successful companies. But you do have to admire the systems, processes, and procedures that they have built to guarantee that the customer always has the same valuable experience.

Chapter 8

Know Your Numbers

Our lives are driven and determined by numbers. We constantly ask ourselves questions such as how many miles is it to drive to, say, London? How many miles do I get per litre of fuel? How much is a litre of fuel? Asking ourselves questions helps us understand the implications of what we're going to do – in this case, how much it will cost to drive to London. When we work it out, we'll probably ask, is it cheaper to go by train? How much and how many are questions constantly on our lips.

Understanding your numbers has a crucial impact on your business. You need to understand the targets, variances and ratios, KPIs, measurement, analysis and the all-important business forecast. Don't panic – you don't need to be an accountant; just ask the questions and use a calculator!

It's your job

Could you pitch to *Dragon's Den* at a minute's notice and convince a Dragon to invest by clearly articulating the numbers? You'll need a good dose of passion, but it's the numbers that investors are really interested in, and not just the accounting financials. Dragons want to know how many customers you have, the size of the market, how many you've sold and at what price, how often customers repeat-purchase, and so on. Too many small businesses often overlook or ignore the numbers and, more importantly, what the numbers are telling them to do. If you don't know the important numbers, your business will drift, unable to make the best decisions.

Countless accountants only look backwards. They're very good at telling you where you went wrong and then they get very excited about your tax position. But you can't run a successful Grown-Up Business only looking backwards. You have to look forwards, sometimes well into the future, sometimes just as far as the next day, week or month. Both are as important as each other: learn from the past to predict and prepare for the future. Look forward to see what's hurtling towards you, but continue to learn how your business performs by looking at what actually happened.

If you were starting a new business today, you could only project the sales you thought you'd achieve in the next month. This would be a combination of your experience, gut feel, and what you'd learnt from your market research. But after just one month of trading, you'd be able to predict the next month's sales with more accuracy. As you complete each month and year in your business, your forecasting ability gets better and better. Your ability to predict improves and you start to forecast your performance.

To be a Grown-Up Business, you need to understand the actual numbers of sales, costs and how much resource or stock you need. Grown-Up Businesses manage by numbers. Even customer feedback can be measured by numbers. Remember "eight out of ten owners said their cat prefers

Whiskas"? Once you start to look at the numbers, you begin to see patterns emerging which will help you forecast the future better. You don't need to be a maths expert: just count and do some simple calculations. Then you'll be able to set realistic and challenging targets, activity levels, and goals to aim for.

Several years ago, I was at a dinner party and a hairdresser was telling me that she wasn't good with numbers. As if to test her, her husband asked her what four times £18 was and she couldn't answer what seemed such a simple question. Her husband then went on to ask her what she would charge for four cuts and blow-dries. She responded instantly with £72. Clearly a cut and blow-dry cost £18. The challenges became more complicated with different combinations of hair treatments, all of which she correctly answered. She knew her numbers, but in a different way. So whatever way works for you is okay; you just have to discover the best formula for you.

As well as knowing your numbers, your role is to know what questions to ask. In our hairdresser's example, you might ask,

- How long does it take a hairdresser to do a cut and blow-dry?
- How many cuts and blow-dries can a hairdresser do each day?
- How many hairdressers do you have in the salon each day?

Those three questions would help you assess…

- the maximum number of customers that you can book in for a cut and blow-dry each day
- the maximum income you can achieve on a given day

So, if a cut and blow-dry takes an hour and each hairdresser works a seven-hour day, then that's seven customers paying £18 each, a total of £126. Now if you have three hairdressers all working the same hours, your maximum income is £378 from 21 customers. If you open six days a week with the same staffing level every day, then your maximum income is £2,268 per week. Now add up all your costs for the year and divide them by 52: you'll end up with your expenses each week. This might be £1,560. This is your breakeven figure. Take away the costs from the income and your gross profit is £708 from 126 customers: £5.61 per customer. All very good, but what if you only have 75 customers booked in or are fully booked already?

Similarly, if we consider a restaurant example, we may well ask,

- How many covers do you have?
- How many lunch and evening services do you have each week?
- What average percentage of covers do you get for each service?
- What is the average spend per cover?

By collecting these numbers, you can see the maximum income potential for the restaurant each week. If you have 50 covers and do six lunch and six dinner services, then you have a maximum potential of 600 diners who spend on average £41 each. This gives an income of £24,600 a week.

But if you only get 30% capacity at lunch sittings, that's 15 covers each lunch. 6 x 15 = 90, so that's 45 lunch covers a week. If you have 75% capacity for evening service, that's 37 covers each dinner. 6 x 37 = 222, so that's 222 covers each dinner. 90 + 222 = 312. You have a total of 312 customers a week with an income of £12,792 per week. Now overlay your breakeven costs to establish your profit.

Once you know the situation, you can make some decisions about what to do. You might decide that you're content with those numbers or decide to increase the number of customers, add some more services, or increase prices. Asking questions helps you make better decisions for your business, because you have facts to inform your thinking.

Numbers can also demonstrate business trends over time. This could be over a year, quarter, month or just a few days or weeks. This graph shows the sales trends for three products.

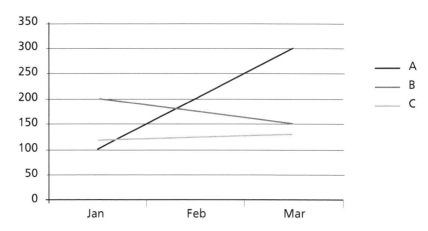

Every picture tells a story and so does this one! Product A is the rising star and I might need to buy more stock soon. Product C is on a downward trend: will this continue? Can I do something to address the downward trend? Product B is growing but oh so slowly. What can I do to increase sales? Do I discontinue this product? If you weren't tracking sales by product and were looking at total income instead, you might not have spotted these trends until it was too late.

I'm not an accountant, never have been, and never will be. But I am interested in numbers: they tell me so much about my business. They quickly highlight where I could do better, where I have a problem, and where the business is doing well.

One of your most important numbers is your breakeven figure. If you don't know that, then you won't know if you've generated enough income to cover your monthly costs. You don't want to suddenly find that you don't have enough money to pay the wages! That's not a nice position to be in and one where the bank manager is no longer as obliging as he used to be. I am always amazed at the blank faces I get when I ask my clients this question. Too many just don't know.

If you don't know your breakeven figure, then it's time to find out.

- ⟳ Add up all your costs (everything you spend – and don't forget your salary) for the past year. Look at the last 12 months so that you include all one-off costs that you might overlook.
- ⟳ Now you have your total figure, divide it by 12 to get your monthly breakeven figure or by 52 for a weekly breakeven figure.
- ⟳ The acid test is this: is your income from sales more than the breakeven figure? If it is, you're on the right track. If not, you need to start making some changes unless you have a very healthy bank balance. Your accountant or bookkeeper will be able to refine this figure further.
- ⟳ If you do have a break even figure, is it time to review it and make sure it's still accurate?
- ⟳ Take your actual sales figures for a selection of your products and plot them onto a graph like the one above. Are the trend lines what you expected? What do you need to address before it becomes a problem?

Lost in translation

Even though I'm not an accountant, I do have to understand some of their language. I have to know the difference between gross and net profit, turnover and revenue, and so on. In the early days, I had to have these explained to me, not in accountancy speak but in my language. I had little notes to remind me which was which. Even today, my online accounts package gives me reminders: "things I sold" and "things I bought" are located directly under the heading of sales and purchase ledger.

If you're dealing with investors, bankers, or accountants you do need to understand the terms that they use. If you're not sure, then double-check and ask them to explain it to you. Talking at cross purposes or assuming you understand can cost you a lot of money.

You know it's all going wrong on *Dragon's Den* when the Dragon starts to drill down into the numbers and the business owner suddenly looks like a rabbit in the headlights. You see it unravelling before your eyes. It's painful to watch. Sadly, it's pretty common when business owners are pitching for investment or to secure a loan or overdraft. Pitches and applications confuse the investor if they use the wrong terms – net profit when you meant gross profit.

Telling the story about your business is important, but it's vital to use the right numbers in the right order. You have to learn and then know your numbers, if you want to be a Grown-Up Business.

Eventually numbers translate into money – your money. If you are a new business, you'll be in boot-strapping mode. Money will be incredibly tight and you'll be watching every penny. It's a good discipline to get into and one that you shouldn't forget too soon. As you start to accumulate money in the business, don't get complacent and don't take your eye off the ball. It's easy to let it seep away or worse still to fritter it away. Cash is king. Profitable businesses go bust because they run out of cash.

Beverly had built a successful business over a number of years. She was confident about her numbers, but less so about the technical words used by the professionals, so she often got flustered. She needed a short-term loan to kickstart another growth phase and spent lots of time working on a plan for the bank. Arriving at the bank, she found her usual manager had been promoted and a new, younger version was in place.

The meeting was a disaster. Beverly was confused by the terms the new bank manager used. When she asked for help, he said, "*Everyone* knows the difference between gross, net profit and EBITDA, what a breakeven point is, and how to do a cash-flow forecast!"

Beverly was shocked by his outburst and lack of help. Her previous bank manager had talked her language, not double Dutch! So she asked him what the difference between a balcony and a plunge was. He had no idea. Beverly was an expert bra fitter; she explained that *everyone* knew the difference between a plunge and a balcony; it was easy!

Up until this point, the whole meeting had been lost in translation; neither side had been speaking the same language. This was a big lesson for both parties. The bank manager soon understood, his attitude changed, and he worked with Beverly to help them both understand better.

Years later, he told Beverly that since that meeting, he always checked what his customer meant when they used financial terms. No more confusion, just greater understanding.

If you feel intimidated by your lack of technical knowledge or language, take time out to learn. Seek help from your bookkeeper, bank manager, and accountant or business expert and try a training course. As we saw in chapter 1, you have to upskill yourself. While you learn, don't assume that you understand; ask to have it explained. If you're nervous about asking, you can always start with, "I know this is probably a silly question, but…"

⮑ Take out your management accounts, profit and loss, and balance sheet and underline everything you aren't sure about. Now find someone who can explain it. If necessary, make your own notes on a master sheet so that you can refer back to it and learn them as you go.

What gets measured gets done

This is always true. You've made sure that you have clear targets and standards, but if you don't measure your actual performance against them, they're meaningless. Once your team knows that you're measuring what is getting done, and how, then they'll make sure that they work on the things that will meet the target. To measure accurately, you need three things: a realistic target, a reliable recording system, and easy, regular reporting.

How often are you pleasantly surprised or thoroughly depressed when you add up the week's takings? Of course, if you don't have a target or track your numbers, it's always going to be a surprise. Surprises aren't always nice; most business people don't like surprises at all.

If you have a target for the week and you're tracking the numbers each day, you'll at least know whether or not you're on target. You might split the week down into daily targets, especially if you have some days during the week that are better trading days than others.

Of course if you don't have sales or production targets, breakeven numbers and a profit figure in mind, you don't have to worry whether or not you've achieved your goals! But leaving everything to happen in the hope that it works out in the end isn't the Grown-Up Business way. So let's see how a Grown-Up Business focuses its attention.

First, you need a realistic target. Some areas you could target include…

- timings for service
    - o answering the phone
    - o responding to e-mails and queries
    - o despatching products
    - o complaint handling
    - o issuing invoices and collecting money
- products
    - o quality control
    - o returns
    - o product complaints
    - o stock levels, using old stock first and making the right things at the right time

- sales
  - o number of calls, visits, pitches, meetings, quotes, and closures
  - o business in the pipeline
  - o repeat purchases and referrals
  - o time between purchases
  - o average order value
  - o upselling, optional extras, maintenance agreements, and so on
- people
  - o absences
  - o customer service standards
  - o learning and training
  - o a reliable recording system

From the five-bar gate ⳾⳾⳾⳾ to online tracking systems, there are many ways to record what's happening. The key is that whichever system you use, it must be reliable. Activity and performance must be recorded regularly, whether that's every day, shift, week, or hour. If you don't have confidence in the reporting system, you won't be any further forward in trying to make better decisions.

The barcode system is fantastic at recording everything from shipments, storage, and delivery to sales – but the whole system becomes pointless if it isn't reported reliably. Confidently recording figures is vital, but it's the reporting that will inform your decision-making. Different industries have different reporting timescales. For example, a bank branch manager will track sales of financial products by the hour. Today, the majority of reporting is online and available via an e-dashboard. Figures are constantly updated to reflect actuals for the period, as well as trends over past periods. How great is it to wake up in the morning, log onto your dashboard, and then decide whether you need to go to work just by looking at the numbers?

Let's revisit Denise at her restaurant to see how numbers influence her activity. She expects Friday and Saturday to be busier than Monday and Tuesday. Every day, she tracks bookings for that day and for the next seven days against her capacity. She now knows how each restaurant is going to perform over the next week and is able to make tactical decisions to maximise her income and profit.

One Tuesday morning, she looked at her bookings and found there were only three bookings for that night, but the rest of the week was looking very good. She had a few choices:

1 close the restaurant (but then she would still have the overheads and no income)
2 open as usual and hope to get some bookings or walk-ins (the expenses remain, but hopefully she gets some additional income)
3 do something to ensure she had more diners that night (expenses remain, but there's an opportunity to maximise profit)

She preferred the third option. She employed some spot marketing by embracing the power of social media with some "tonight only" offers. This is where numbers raise their head again: how many contacts did she have on her email list, how many Twitter and or Facebook followers? Effectively, what was her marketing reach? She offered a free bottle of wine for that night only to her followers and soon bookings were on the up.

By using social and online media, Denise also gave herself the opportunity to track the results of her efforts. How many people responded, booked for that night (or another night), and signed up for her newsletter? The next time she needed to do something to improve bookings, she'd be able to make an even better decision on the marketing tactics she should use and estimate the likely results. How grown up is that?

Of course in this whole scenario, she also needed to know the restaurant's numbers very well. Her choice of tactic would have been very different if she knew that on average they had 22 walk-ins every Tuesday night.

Knowing the numbers helps you to make the best decision at the right time. Decision-making by gut reaction is not a Grown-Up Business decision.

- ⮑ Think about the sales process for your business. Take the sales target for the next month, then divide it by the number of days, shifts, or sessions to get a daily target.
- ⮑ You might have higher sales on certain days of the week. If so, adjust daily numbers, keeping the overall target the same.
- ⮑ What is the average sales value per order? Divide the total days by the average sales value to get the number of sales you require each day.
- ⮑ Are these targets realistic, recorded, and reported?
- ⮑ This is your target for tomorrow or next week: tell everyone. Track your performance and adjust the target as required. These calculations are also crucial for the forecasting section later in this chapter.

Key Performance Indicators (KPIs)

As you begin to understand the power of knowing your numbers it's easy to try to measure, track and predict too many. You end up paralysed, unable to make any decisions. That's why Grown-Up Businesses have KPIs. These are the crucial numbers that you should be setting, recording, reporting, and tracking on a regular basis. By their very description they are important and there won't be many of them. (If you have lots of indictors, they can't all be the key ones!) Depending on your business, you might be reviewing these KPIs daily, weekly, monthly or even hourly.

There are all sorts of numbers that could be KPIs. Deciding which are the most important is crucial. For example, if you're an e-commerce business, you might track the number of orders placed before midday that must be despatched before 4 pm. You wouldn't be so interested in footfall at your warehouse or telephone calls.

At the start of a new business venture, you select the key numbers to track. Over time, these may change; you may wish to track the number of product returns or complaints. By all means, add new KPIs to your list, but don't keep adding numbers on a whim. Select the important ones. Your KPI list should contain no more than a dozen. If you have more, you need to review the list and reduce it. Keep the list short or you'll end up recording everything – so much information that you become blinded to the areas that need your attention.

As the business grows and you establish departments, each department should have its own numbers to make sure it's performing at its highest level. A limited list helps your managers quickly spot where there might be a problem that needs solving.

Reporting departmental KPIs upwards and sideways in the business helps you and your senior management team react and solve problems as a team. For example, if you're manufacturing widgets and the customer services team are flooded with calls for extra orders, you might have to increase production – but you might also consider raising prices or removing bulk discount. Conversely, if you suddenly find orders have dried up or are being cancelled, you might have a quality issue, delivery might be a problem or a competitor might have suddenly launched a new, better product or discount. Getting a quick heads-up that something has changed gives you the very best opportunity to address it quickly, before the business suffers.

It's not just the things that go wrong that help you improve your business, although these are valuable pointers to problem solving. It's also the good things, the successes and upward trends that allow you to plan to meet future growth. A sudden upturn in sales indicates that you probably need more resources, stock, and capacity.

Using KPIs can identify trends in the business. If you're struggling to decide which numbers should be KPIs, then try breaking them down into categories. These could include sales, cash, and profit.

Sales trends provide lots of market intelligence about your competitors, your customers' confidence in you, your products, and your service.

Money trends tell you about your cash position. Remember that profitable businesses go bust if they run out of cash. These KPIs tell you about funding requirements or investment opportunities, how good your credit control is, how much you owe and when it's due, especially your tax obligations.

Profit margins are important KPIs too, whether they are by product line, stock keeping units (SKUs), or range. Understanding which products make, lose, or breakeven for profit is a good yardstick to refine your product offering. You might consider some of the following questions:

- What are your most and least profitable products?

- Which customers contribute the most and least profit?
- How can you improve margins?
- How are package products performing?
- Which route to market is most profitable for you?

Knowing KPIs helps Grown-Up Businesses answer the bigger questions, such as...

- When will we need to find bigger premises, additional outlets, start exporting, and so on?
- Do we need to adjust our staffing up or down? Do we need different skills or staff in new places?
- Do we need to buy more stock, materials, components, or storage capacity? Should we consider outsourcing our pick-and-pack warehousing or bring it in house? Could we offer pick-and-pack facilities for other companies?
- Do we need to update our accounting and management systems? Is it time to move into the cloud? Is our data secure enough? What customer data do we need to hold?

Luke and Simon's company manufactures and supplies products to festivals, sporting events, and large social gatherings. They had just taken over from their dad as the second generation of the family business. Their business was growing; they had big plans to attract more customers, increase sales, and grow cash in the bank. Great – but they didn't know which products or customers were profitable. Nor did they know the average order values, breakeven points, debtor days, or overdue debtors. In fact, their only checkpoint each month was whether cash at the bank had increased and how stressed the team were!

It was complicated: they had hundreds of product variations with lots of customers ordering all sorts of products. Luke and Simon were struggling to make the best business decisions, because they were always taking a stab in the dark, keeping fingers crossed and hoping for the best. They also discovered that they'd outgrown their accounting system. This was the perfect opportunity to get a grip of the situation. They set up a project to upgrade the accounting system and establish the key numbers for their business. This would inform future strategy.

They assigned product codes and set up a price list and a margin range. Customer accounts were tidied up and orders were linked to accounts, along with payment histories. Not only did they record numbers via the accounting system, they started tracking other numbers too: product returns, quality performance, delays, repeat purchase cycles, complaints. They also tracked calls on the phone system and analysed information gathered from the website and their online business. They learnt so much.

They defined a set of 11 KPIs. These would be the dashboard which Luke and Simon would use to manage the business. It was a long process; they had 30 years of information, systems, and data to organise. Nonetheless, they succeeded in extracting lots of valuable information to analyse the business. Gaps were uncovered and plugged; business started to accelerate, as did the cash in the bank.

Today, they can direct the business from the dashboard. They have realistic targets and a clear business and cash flow forecast, and have made even more money. How? They dealt with underperforming products and customers, and reduced a lot of unnecessary expenses.

- ⊃ Pull out your current management information reports. Yes, every one of them! I expect that you have lots of these.
- ⊃ From the section above, think about which KPIs are important in sales, cash, and profit.
- ⊃ Now reflect on the questions that you ask your team regularly. These must be important, so they need to go on to your KPI list.
- ⊃ Get the expert who runs your accounting software to show you what information you could have and decide if it's important to you.
- ⊃ Decide how often you need to know the numbers; set out your reporting timetable.
- ⊃ These KPIs and the frequency can be put into an e-dashboard, so it's available anywhere.

Targets, tolerances, variances, and ratios

Numbers don't lie: they are what they are and you can't change them. You can interpret them, analyse them, and calculate them, but whatever you do with the numbers, be truthful to yourself and everyone else. Changing numbers only deceives you and no one else. It's important to you, your investor or shareholders, your bank, and your team that you're truthful about the numbers. Poetic licence should only be employed to interpret them, but use this carefully. Remember your moral and legal obligations.

As we've seen, setting SMART targets is the first step to building a Grown-Up Business. SMART targets are Specific, Measurable, Achievable, Relevant, and Targeted (or Timed). If you don't know what you're trying to achieve, you'll never get there – but there's no point saying you're going to treble sales in the next three months if that's not achievable.

The *target* is a defined number that you will hit on its head, drop short of, or exceed. The *tolerance* that you're prepared to accept, over or under the target figure, gives you your *range*. Your *variance* is the amount by which you miss the target number.

For example, your *target* for debtor days might be 38 days. Your *tolerance* is one day either way, giving you a *range* of 37 to 39. If the actual reported figure is between these numbers, then all is well and no action is required. However, if the reported numbers fall outside the range, this is the *variance*. Then you need to consider what to do. A variance is an early-warning system that requires your urgent attention. You might also want to consider what to do if the target figure is dropping by a small amount every month. This would indicate a downward trend.

If your profit margin is 32% and your tolerance is two percentage points up and one percentage point down, then performance within the range 31% to 34% is fine. Outside of that range and you need to pay attention.

As well as actual numbers, you also need to understand ratios and how they impact your business. A *ratio* is the proportional relationship between two different numbers or quantities.

To explain why ratios are important, let's look at sales ratios. You'll need to know how many leads you must achieve to hit your sales targets. Each business will have its own sales processes but a typical B2B sales process might look like this: enquiry, then meeting, then quote, then sale (not forgetting repeat sales!).

A typical ratio throughout the sales process is 3 to 1. So for every three enquiries you have, you'll get one meeting. For every three meetings you have, you'll get one quote, and so on.

3 to 1 is a good benchmark to start with, but track and record your actual performance to see where you're performing well and areas where you need to improve. You can then use the actual benchmarks to set your desired target and start working on improvements.

This table shows a sale process and its conversion ratios. The first column shows the typical conversion rates, with three different examples of how it actually went.

	Typical 3 to 1	Example A	Example B	Example C
Enquiries	100	100	100	100
Meetings	33	10	33	50
Quotes	11	8	6	26
Sales	4	7	1	1

In Example A, they have a 10 to 1 enquiries-to-meetings ratio, a 1.25 to 1 meetings-to-quotes ratio, and almost a 1 to 1 quotes-to-sales ratio. What does that tell you? Perhaps...

1 The wrong people might be enquiring.
2 You're failing to convert enquiries into meetings – but why?
3 Your performance at meetings is good: you're meeting the right people and you have a great solution to their problem.
4 Your quotes are either hitting the buyer's buttons or you might be too cheap.

In example B, we can see a different picture. The enquiries-to-meetings ratio is the expected 3 to 1. The meetings-to-quotes ratio is much worse: almost 6 to 1. The quotes-to-sales ratio is equally bad, at 6 to 1 again.

1   You have the expected level of enquiries to meetings.
2   You have a poor performance on quotes: you're not solving clients' problems at meetings or you're not seeing the decision-makers. Perhaps you're not asking for the opportunity to quote.
3   Your quote-to-sales ratio is equally poor, so you need to discover (really discover) why you're not winning quotes.

In example C, we see totally different strengths and weaknesses. The enquiries-to-meetings ratio is a very strong 2 to 1. The meetings-to-quotes ratio is also great, just above 2 to 1. But the quotes-to-sales ratio is appalling, at 26 to 1!

1   You're fantastic at getting meetings – but are they with the right people?
2   A 2 to 1 meeting-to-quote ratio is good, but are they getting you out of the door by asking for a quote even though they don't want one?
3   Your quote-to-sales definitely says something is wrong. This needs your attention now.

Time for a little homework.

⮑ Gather all your sales figures together over a period. You're going to establish a benchmark of your actual performance.
⮑ Using the table above, add your own numbers and calculate the ratios between your numbers. Your business might have additional steps in the sales process. If so, add these in as well.
⮑ Are you hitting the 3:1 ratio? Are you better in some areas than others?
⮑ Identify where the numbers are telling you that you have a problem and work towards finding a solution to improve your sales performance ratios.

Are you paying people to buy from you?

Based on Pareto's principle, 20% of your products will deliver 80% of your profit and 20% of your customers or clients will help deliver 80% of your profit. Not every customer is profitable. Customers are the lifeblood of any business, but too many of the wrong type of customer will signal the death knell for your business.

When you start a business it's tempting to take on every client that comes your way. It doesn't matter whether or not they're ideal or a money-making client. In those early days, we just celebrate winning clients, but many of them will end up costing you a lot of money to deal with in the future.

A client who is profitable for single transaction should be even more profitable when they repeat-purchase from you. After all, you haven't had to spend any money to get them as a client. Your profit margin should increase. Depending on your industry, market, and customer base, you should be able to target the amount of repeat business that you should secure in the future.

One school of thought is that you actively seek to sack your bottom 10% of loss-making or low-profit clients. The argument goes that if you remove these time-wasting, resource-draining clients, you'll have more time to focus on replacing them with more profitable clients. Just take a moment to think about your difficult clients or customers.

- the one that screws you on price and then doesn't pay on time
- the never-satisfied one – complaining, returning goods, and generally causing havoc
- the "I need you to just…" one, who always wants you to bend over backwards for them
- the threatening one – "I'll go elsewhere if you don't…"
- the 24/7 one, always calling out of hours
- the one that ruins your day, the one you dread having to talk to

We all have unprofitable clients or customers; we're just really bad at accepting it or doing anything about it. You can't argue with the numbers. They prove how much you're losing per client, as they chew up your valuable resources and stop you focusing on finding and working with your most important, best, and most inspiring clients.

So how do you make the step change in your business? Sack the bad ones, professionally of course. You may think, *I can't afford to lose the income!* I say that you can't afford to keep them. They cost you money every day and stop you from making more money from better clients.

Mike Michalowicz's book, *The Pumpkin Plan* (a great read by the way!), talks about clearing out the bad clients and how to focus on getting more of your top clients. You need to take a critical look at all your clients. Making a list in descending order of revenue is a good starting point.

The numbers will help you to establish how often a customer would typically repeat-purchase from you. For example, if you're selling dog food, customers might buy from you every week, but if you're selling hats, it might only be two or three times a year. Understanding the number of repeat purchases and the percentage of customers that do repeat-purchase will help you plan forward to next year. Add to that the opportunity cost for referrals and recommendations. You can then calculate the lifetime value of your customer.

John runs a commercial insurance brokerage. Many clients have been with him for over 25 years. They love the service, but most of all they love his superb technical knowledge. They all know they have an expert in their corner.

John's new clients come from word-of-mouth recommendations, which is how he got Sarah. He bent over backwards to make sure that she understood her insurance contract and was always happy to help. For the first couple of years, the account ran smoothly, but Sarah's business was expanding rapidly and she was starting to lose control. She cancelled meetings with John, left everything to the last minute, overlooked invoices and paperwork, and then ended up calling him in a panic. She didn't listen to his advice, she let the spinning plate crash to the ground, and then she found herself in all sorts of trouble.

John helped her out, but she was unable to get her business under control. After she made a number of unreasonable phone calls and threats to move her business, he suggested that finding another supplier was indeed a very good idea. The relief for him and his team was enormous. The extra time they saved was ploughed into delivering an even better service to their best clients.

If you're in John's situation, then ask yourself these questions:

- Do you really make any money or profit out of this client?

- How much "free" work do you end up doing just because they shout the loudest?
- What is the real impact on you, your team, and your other clients?
- What would your business and your life be like without this client?

It's time to review your client list.

- ➲ Put off a full client list and your accounting system in revenue order, largest at the top.
- ➲ Consider the six types of undesirables as you go through the list. A red pen to cross them off is very useful!
- ➲ Review the list again and consider those who actively refer or recommend you, so you can earn more money.
- ➲ You should have 10% of your clients on the red list.
- ➲ Meet your top clients and find out what else you could do to serve them better.
- ➲ If you're not sure about some of them, think about how you could improve the profitability of these customers.

All the clients on your red list need to be moved on, so this is how to sack a client – professionally, of course. First you need to make sure that you've considered all the options. Then, if you decide that the best option is to move them on, these are the points to consider.

- Check the contract – don't breach it; work within the terms and conditions.
- Set out your reasons so that you have clearly thought them through. You can use these as notes for the meeting, but only for you to see!
- Set up a face-to-face meeting with the client – you owe them that.
- Talk to the client to explain the situation clearly and firmly.
- Establish your 100% win and calmly, carefully win your client over to moving on.
- Establish a phased withdrawal or date to cease the relationship, depending on your type of business.
- No personal comments are allowed, to anyone, ever.
- Help the client to make a smooth transition to their new supplier.
- Finally, sit down and assess what you've learnt from the whole process.

Now with the extra time and resources on your hands, go and find the right clients and put a smile on your face instead of a frown!

What's the forecast?

Hardly any business owners that I meet have a business forecast. Some have a cash-flow forecast, but that's about it. At least with a cash-flow forecast, they can track cash, and that's important, but how do you manage a growing business without a forecast? How do you secure debt or equity funding without a forecast? How do you know if you're going to deliver projects on time, make money, or even stay in business without a forecast? In my experience, with great difficultly. Now that you've got a clear idea of your numbers, your KPIs, and your targets, tolerances, variances, and ratios, it's time to see how a business forecast will help you keep on track.

Grown-Up Businesses are fantastic at anticipating future trends and problems, and then delivering a successful outcome: their dream. The very best tool to help you is the business forecast. It'll keep you aiming at your targets and goals, and make sure that you stay on track. You need a forecast. A Growing-Up Business forecast covers everything from sales to cash through to production, stock, capacity, resources, and timescales. You can monitor what's happening, adjust as required, and maximise business performance, sales, and profit. Make money, save time, and reduce stress.

From my work with small and medium enterprises (SMEs), it's clear most businesses aren't sure how to prepare a forecast, nor are they comfortable with managing the business against the forecast. Even a reforecast can prove very difficult for them and unfortunately there isn't much help at hand. Even bank managers expect you to know how to do a forecast, yet sadly most can't help you beyond supplying a template.

Once you know how, it isn't hard to construct a robust forecast that, if used regularly, can really help you make better, grown-up decisions. The business may burn lots of cash as it starts to grow successfully, so your forecast is essential: it gives you foresight.

You'll need to include…

- sales / revenue by product stream – either monetary or unit, whichever is easiest
- capacity and resources – these will vary each month; even a holiday chart can help
- cash – money in and money out (regular and ad hoc)
- stockholding – minimum and maximum levels
- margins – product and profit
- capital expenditure – growth and investment cash
- new products, launches, major events and timelines
- marketing activity

An Excel spreadsheet is a good starting point. Remember, your forecast is no good unless you use it. It's a waste of time preparing a forecast if you don't review your actual performance against the forecast each week or each month, and adjust your tactics as necessary. Each time you complete a month, add it on to the next year's forecast, so if you've finished July, then add July next year to your forecast.

Rufus needed a business forecast to show his bank manager that he could service the loan he was applying for. He'd never done one before, so he enlisted the help of his accountant. Instead of preparing the forecast for him, she asked him loads of questions – just the same questions that a Dragon would ask. She wanted lots of numbers so that she could populate the spreadsheet.

Rufus soon realised that his accountants couldn't help him much: she didn't know enough about his business, but he did. He pulled out his monthly management reports and compiled his year-to-date figures for each line of the accounts. Next, he took the year-to-date figures and projected those forward, adding 20% to every number to take into account his growth plans. He did the same for the following year too, then he adjusted the numbers account for the new products that he planned to launch and the extra costs he knew he'd incur.

Once he'd put the forecast together, it started to raise all sorts of questions about his future projections. What if he did better than we thought or sales collapsed? I suggested to Rufus that he needed three versions of his forecast: realistic, pessimistic, and optimistic. We copied the spreadsheets over, then flexed the number to give us the three different projections.

Within the business community, everyone talks about the need for three- or five-year plans. Yes, you do need a longer-term plan, but your main focus must be on the near future. It's like the weather forecast; the next five days is pretty accurate, next month a bit iffy, next season is more of a theme and further out it's totally unpredictable! I love this graphic designed by Dog House Diaries (www.doghousediaries.com) – it speaks for itself!

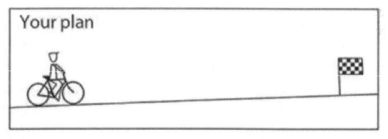

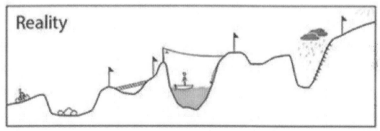

With this graphic in mind, you'll now understand why a three-version business forecast is vital. In nearly all cases, the actual performance of the business will fall somewhere between the pessimistic and optimistic projections. The discipline and skill of a Grown-Up Business owner is to keep reforecasting monthly, if not weekly, to make sure that you know where your sales are coming from and what your costs are.

That said, don't think that you can ignore the long term goals. Use them to dictate your short term goals. Start with the endgame in mind, your five year goals and set that in stone. You also know where you are now so you have both ends of the line.

For example, your current turnover is £1.2 million and your five year goal is £7 million. Perhaps your staged turnover goals look like this? The chart below is just an example. It is unlikely that every growth line will be a straight line going from bottom left to top right – it does happen, but expect your growth to be more like a staircase; periods of growth followed by short periods of consolidation (the stair tread).

Current Year	Year 1	Year 2	Year 3	Year 4	Year 5
1.2M	2M	3.2M	4.8M	6M	7M

The next task is to breakdown Year 1 into months or quarters, to give you a set of smaller short term goals. Therefore in Year 1 you need to turnover £2 million so each quarter's target might be £500,000 or each month £170,000. Naturally many businesses are seasonal, so you'll need to reflect the shape of your business over the year. Your focus is now to deliver the target for the next month or quarter. What do you have to do to increase sales from £100,000 (current performance) to £170,000, your targeted performance? How many repeat customers, how many new customers and how will you find them? How much stock, capacity or resources do you need? These are all the types of questions you will need to ask.

⊃ If you don't have a business forecast, start to prepare one, even if it's only for the next three or six months. Without it, you won't have anything to measure your performance against or an early-warning system when the business starts to over- or underperform. Just as Rufus did, you can start by using last year's actual numbers from your monthly management accounts to forecast forward.

⊃ Diarise your reforecast: I suggest monthly at best and quarterly at worst.

Building your first forecast will take time, but each time you reforecast you'll become more proficient, quicker, and more accurate too.

Let's return to *Dragon's Den*. A mediocre product with great people behind it will fly higher than a fantastic product with a mediocre team. Dragons want to invest in companies that they can scale up. They want to be able to see this in the numbers that are in your business forecast. If you aren't projecting your sales and expenses going forward, how can you expect to assess whether or not those numbers are realistic.

One of the biggest causes of business failures is buying that posh car before it is really affordable. Yes it makes a statement but an even bigger statement if it sends your business under. Understand where you are earning the most and least income, as well as where you are losing money. Just because the bank balance looks healthy doesn't mean that it's all your money. Remember the bills you have to pay.

Make sure that you know who is spending your money and what they are spending it on. It's always easier to spend other people's money with less care than you would your own. So put some guidelines and limits in place for your team, alongside the purchase order process.

Remember that as a business owner you have a moral obligation to trade responsibly. This extends to your suppliers, customers, staff, your family and your community. In most cases you also have a legal responsibility to ensure that you are trading solvently and it's the numbers that will make sure you do.

Chapter 9

Solve Problems, Permanently

Starting a business is relatively easy, but running and growing a high-performing company is a real challenge – one that only 6% of companies manage to achieve. Success is all about achieving your objectives, the SMART goals you set. Grown-Up Businesses are super-successful because they always achieve their objectives. How? They remove any and all of the obstacles that are holding them back. That means solving problems that present themselves as obstacles.

Ignore problems at your peril. They can derail your business, sending you crashing into the buffers, usually when you least expect it! Some companies hit the buffers with an almighty and fatal crash; others have a big bump which they may or may not survive. The rest (and I mean everyone else) will be lucky and just give the buffers a nudge. Whatever impact you have with the buffers, it's not fun. It's painful, stressful, demoralising, and depressing, but it's avoidable.

In this chapter we'll look at why you shouldn't be firefighting, how to seek out problems, and the Nine Essential Skills of Problem Solving.

The majority of business owners start companies because they have a technical skill, a passion or a hobby that they turn into a business. Some are just great at spotting an opportunity to start a business – the entrepreneurs. But what the majority of business owners don't have, or aren't even aware that they need, is a toolkit of management skills that has nothing to do with their technical competence or expertise. One of those key skills is problem solving. If you don't learn and develop this skill, it could have serious consequences for your company.

I know and have seen throughout my business career and my work in a wide range of industries and diverse companies the damage that failing to solve problems causes:

- lost money – sometimes lots of it
- wasted time and resources, which in turn loses even more money
- high stress levels – that's not good for anyone
- ill health, or worse
- divorce
- loss of the pleasure or fun in running a business, which was set up with such huge passion and hope
- disappointed customers, who are sometimes out of pocket and certainly inconvenienced
- abandoned staff and the negative impact on families and the local community
- frustrated suppliers, shareholders, and so on

Throughout my career, solving problems has become my forte. It was the problem solving that I missed when I tried to retire. (I failed!) Now, in my work with business owners, it's the problem-solving skill set that is most in demand. I've designed and developed the Nine Essential Skills of Problem Solving to help all business owners do a much better job of problem solving. My strategy is that if you *really* solve it, if you take time to make sure the solution is the right one, you'll never have to deal with it again. The alternative is to be caught up in the endless loop of firefighting.

Firefighting is such hard work

Many business owners spend all day every day firefighting. They successfully move one problem off their desk only to see it replaced with another one – one which, ironically, they've seen before. The sad part is that very few of the problems that business owners deal with each day are unique. They've all happened before, but they're never really solved. All the problem ever gets is a sticky plaster, instead of the plaster cast that the problem requires to treat it correctly.

In Sam Carpenter's *Work the System*, he calls this scenario "whacking moles". As a mole pops its head above ground, you whack it on the head and it goes away. But it's only a temporary solution; the mole will pop up again and again. In the end, there are so many moles popping up all over the place that it fills your day. You're exhausted and you dread tomorrow, when it will start all over again.

We all know of businesses that have ceased trading for whatever reason – some voluntarily, many not so. We also know that many companies go bust because they run out of cash, but in most cases that isn't the real cause. Here are some possible underlying reasons:

- It was much too late when they finally became aware of the problem.
- They have found the problem, but actively ignored it – the "it won't happen to me" syndrome.
- They failed to address the real problems, perhaps because they were distracted by dealing with the symptoms.
- They lacked the skills, commitment, or leadership to actually solve the problem.
- They allowed a problem to escalate out of control.

All of these actions, or lack of them, can be avoided. You have a choice. If you want to avoid that bump with the buffers, then you'll need to develop your problem solving skills to be able to avoid the crash.

"The measure of success is not whether you had a tough problem to deal with, but whether it is the same problem you had last year," said John Foster Dulles, Former Secretary of State. That sums up the situation brilliantly.

Naturally, when you're working hard to solve problems, your time is fully employed. You have little time to think about future opportunities. You don't have time to spot them or to take advantage of them when they come along. Not only are you losing out on new opportunities to accelerate your business growth, you are running hard just to stand still at best. Ignoring those problems means that your business will continue to…

- waste time
- delay achieving your objectives
- see stress, tension, and time off work increase and production fall
- waste precious resources

This costs the business more money: time spent doing non-productive things as well as money spent focusing on the wrong thing.

Grown-Up Businesses consistently work through their problems, right down to the root cause. They strive to solve the problem once and for all. The goal is never to have to deal with the same problem ever again. They dedicate time to this and focus on really solving the problem, so that they save lots of time and money in the future.

Mark and John run a professional practice in the construction industry. Both of them are technicians and excellent at what they do, but they're always looking for new sales and clients. They have lots of meetings and issue lots of quotes, but just never seem to win the business. They positioned themselves as "experts in their field"; it says that on their website. They're not the most expensive and they do deliver results but sales are still tough.

I suggested some research with clients – a quick dipstick test. When they were talking to clients, I told them to ask each client, at the end of the conversation, "What three words would you use to describe our company?" They didn't do what I suggested; instead, they emailed all their clients and asked the same question.

The point of the telephone call was to get an instant reaction from the client, rather than a carefully considered response, which wasn't going to be as helpful. Few responded, but the responses they did receive held the key to their problem.

For example, one client said they were "competent". I asked Mark and John how they felt about this. "Pretty neutral," they said. I explained that they positioned themselves as experts; a "competent" rating wasn't good enough. All sorts of excuses followed. I suggested a call to the responder, to dig a little deeper and find out why they were only competent. It didn't happen for ages. In Mark and John's mind, poor sales was the salesman's fault.

They had the perfect opportunity to discover the root cause of their sales problems, but they ignored it. The situation deteriorated until the pain was enough for them to act. When they did talk to their clients, they discovered why they hadn't been rated as expert. As a result, they changed the way they served clients, the offers that they made, and the quality of their work, together with added-value services. This enabled them to complete more sales and get their business moving forward.

➲ What problems have you dealt with in the last six months?
➲ What did you do to solve them?
➲ Which ones had you dealt with before?
➲ How much did it cost you not to solve the problem and how much will dealing with the same problem again cost you?
➲ Are your team delegating problem solving to you?

Why can't we solve the problem?

If you're dealing with the same problem again today, then you weren't able to solve it yesterday. You were so pleased to get it off your desk that you didn't reflect on why you didn't get it right last time. We tend to repeat what we did before and that, sadly, will give us exactly the same result.

Sometimes the solution you put in place isn't the right one. A challenge for all business owners is to continually improve the business. That means revisiting the problem again, to ensure that it really is solved and if not, to tweak the solution again and again until it is really solved. That is the grown-up way of getting to really good solutions.

Sadly, most businesses don't solve the problem because it's easier to ignore it today. But eventually you do have to deal with it; you won't have a choice! Here are 11 possible reasons why you haven't solved the problem:

1   Misinterpreting or misunderstanding the problem
Perhaps you think the problem is one thing, but instead it's a combination of two or three other things.

2   Procrastinating
Many people procrastinate because they don't know what to do, so they don't do anything. They're indecisive, and so delay making what is sometimes an obvious move. Alternately, they fear the consequences of making the wrong move.

3   Solving the problem too quickly – not a thorough diagnosis
Being fleet of foot is a key trait of many up-and-coming businesses, but making quick decisions with little information is a bad thing. We're so desperate to get the problem off our back that we look for the easiest part to solve, instead of taking time to really understand it.

4   Solving the problem superficially
You need to get to the root of the problem. I was meeting a friend at a country pub recently and she said, "If you think you're lost, just keep going and you'll find it." The same is true for problems: keep digging until you get to the bottom of the problem.

5 Not committing to change

Part of your leadership is being committed to change, to drive the problem solving. Jeff Bezos has a clear commitment to change and this is at the heart of Amazon's success. You have to drive the problem-solving work ethic in your company.

6 Avoiding conflict by ignoring it

Solving a problem can mean that it's someone's fault and they need to know. Most people avoid this conflict, but failing to address the issue with people won't help you solve the problem.

7 Abdicating the implementation

By all means delegate, but don't abdicate. "It's your fault, you sort it out," is an outdated management approach. When you delegate, follow up to make sure the problem is solved.

8 Lack of knowledge, attitude, skills, and habits

If your team's guessing what to do next, that's never very successful. They tend to give up or end up wasting lots of time on the wrong things. Having a process and method in place to guide everyone in the business is essential.

9 External influences

These could be anything from government to nature. Don't give up and don't become a victim.

10 Internal Politics – them and us – departmental silos

This is a hugely destructive culture and one where you as the business owner need to show the way. Introduce collaborative working and project teams to break down the silos and stop the blame game.

11 Poor communication, blockages

Clear communication is always a challenge for companies. It seems the corporate jungle drums work much better than any official communication!

I love this quote from Peter Drucker: "Erroneous assumptions can be disastrous." Assuming that someone else will deal with the problem or just hoping it will go away could be fatal.

Problems, outcomes, symptoms, or causes

Put simply, a problem is anything that stops you achieving your goal. It's an obstacle that you must overcome. You have to understand right from the beginning that every problem has a root cause (the bit you have to solve) and an outcome (which is often mistaken for the problem). Nine times out of ten, what you think the problem is isn't the real problem. Most people solve the outcomes rather than the actual cause, the apparent problem not the actual problem. The visible part gets the attention, rather than the cause. But solving the outcome of the problem is only ever a short-term fix, because the problem comes back again and again. You need to solve the cause.

To illustrate what I mean, I'd like to share this true story with you: The Soapbox Problem. As part of my research, I discovered this case study on numerous websites, with identical wordings explaining the situation. What was different was how each website had taken the example and added its own questions to the end of the piece. So let me share the story with you first.

One of the most memorable problem-solving case studies is the case of the empty soapbox. This is what happened in one of Japan's biggest cosmetics companies. The company received a complaint that a consumer had bought a soapbox that was empty. Immediately, the authorities isolated the problem to the assembly line, which transported all the packaged boxes of soap to the delivery department. For some reason, one soapbox went through the assembly line empty. Management asked its engineers to solve the problem.

Post-haste, the engineers worked hard to devise an X-ray machine with high-resolution monitors manned by two people to watch all the soapboxes that passed through the line to make sure they were not empty. No doubt they worked hard and they worked fast, but they spent a huge amount to do so. But when a rank-and-file employee in a small company was posed with the same problem, he did not get into the complications of X-rays, et cetera, but instead came out with another solution. He bought a strong industrial electric fan and pointed it at the assembly line. He switched the fan on and as each soapbox passed the fan, it simply blew the empty boxes out of the line.

That's the story as it's published online. The oldest entry I can source is from Techinasia (www.techinasia.com/remove-empty-soapboxes/) which states "original source of story undetermined". Many website and commentators will tell you that it's always the simplest solution that solves the problem: don't try to over complicate the solution. Let's take this empty soap box case study to consider the real problem.

- Firstly, a Grown-Up Business wouldn't allow its customers to be its quality control department – that's hardly the approach of a Grown-Up Business.
- They didn't uncover all the facts. For example, how many empty boxes had been dispatched? When did it happen and when was the problem discovered? And the biggest question of all should have been, "What caused it? *Why* did it happen?"
- Because they didn't identify the real problem, the soap box company jumped to the wrong solution: check if the boxes are empty. They should have been solving why the soap hadn't been put into the box in the first place.
- The root cause was in the assembly line, not the delivery department. If they'd gone back over the problem again, they would have discovered this. This is where the soapbox company failed: they didn't solve the right problem.
- The real questions and correction plan should have been something like this:
  o Why doesn't the soap go into every box in the assembly line?
  o What steps do we need to correct to make sure soap is packed into every box?
  o When do we need the solution implemented?
  o Who is doing the changes, alterations, and actions?
  o Where are corrections being applied to the process and the new system?
  o How will we test that the new solution is effective?

Many of the online comments and observations attributed to the case study focus on always looking for simple solutions. My advice is to make sure that you are solving the *real* problem before you look for the simplest solution.

Expert problem solving isn't a recognised qualification, but wow is it important! Once you master the art of identifying the real problem, being committed to resolving it and having a clear approach and method to help you, then you can help your business grow up step by step. You want fire prevention rather than firefighting; grabbing opportunities rather than realising they've passed you by.

Attack a problem now: solve it so that you never have to solve it again. It'll take a little time, but what an investment, because you'll save so much more time and money later on. And your customers will love your consistently consistent approach so much that they will buy and recommend more.

Megan, my writing coach, had been solving the outcome of a particular problem for years and she'd wasted lots of time, energy, and money solving what she thought the problem was. After critiquing this section of the book, she shared her thoughts with me.

As well as delivering one-to-one non-fiction coaching, she runs fiction writing workshops and courses. When it came time for each course, it was never full. So with a big last-minute panic, some expensive short term advertising, and an injection of dedicated effort, Megan filled the next course. But she'd been putting in this extra effort and spending extra money on and off for the past three years to make sure that her courses were full.

This was…

- stressful – would she have enough paying students?
- disruptive – she had to stop doing something else to focus on marketing
- time-wasting – she had to Photoshop each advert with the new dates, et cetera
- expensive – as short bursts of concentrated marketing and advertising cost more

Megan realised that she had been whacking the same mole for years, wasting so much time, money, and effort. It was time to solve the real problem once and for all. But what was the underlying problem? It was the sporadic, ad hoc, and rushed advertising. And the problem under that? She didn't have time, so her adverts arrived late or she forgot to place them. She talked to the advertisers and discovered a few things:

- They would do the Photoshop work for her.
- The cost per advertisement reduced when she had an advert running all the time – the annual total was actually cheaper than the individual costs for each panic advert.
- All Megan needed to supply was the initial artwork and a list of dates and venues for future courses: they'd take care of the rest.
- It was much less stressful, as new students were signing up all the time, so she always had a full course to look forward to.

Megan's world changed dramatically. She'd saved lots of time, because the advertisers were now doing it all. The money spent was working much harder and was less than she had been paying. With the time saved, she could have some free time to herself or use it to move the business forward. Her stress levels remained low – no last minute-panics. Instead, she had a steady stream of new students.

To solve your real problems once and for all, you need the Nine Essential Skills of Problem Solving.

Nine Essential Skills of Problem Solving

You can't solve a problem with the same thinking that created it. Knowing that you've solved the real problem is a great place to be – a wonderful, satisfying feeling that you won't ever have to whack that mole again! Problem solving is challenging, though, and it's not always easy. If it were, everyone would be doing it, but they're not – and that's why their businesses aren't making any progress.

Many business owners don't realise the huge benefits of having clear systems and processes in their company and just as many have failed to understand the real benefits of great problem solving. Problem-solving skills just haven't registered with many. This section introduces you to a robust process that guarantees that you can solve problems. It will be hard work in the short term, but the rewards are huge.

When you realise something is wrong, this model directs you to work through it systematically, solving the problem once and for all. Your business will soon become leaner, meaner, fitter, and stronger, and of course you'll be making more money. Even solving just one problem will make all the difference.

These are the Nine Essential Skills of Problem Solving:

Nine Essential Skills of Problem Solving

To understand and work the model you move clockwise around the circle. Let's explore each box in order while remembering the format. As we move through this model, we will return to Frances at The Clipper NoteBook Company and we'll follow her through a problem solving scenario.

1. Be aware - Something's wrong

Problems can be sudden or slow-developing, expected or unexpected, hidden or visible, detected or unknown, complex or simple: by nature they are consistently inconsistent! This means that your antennae must be working all the time, gathering information and becoming aware of what's happening or might happen.

You need to develop the awareness skill much as you do when you're driving: anticipating speed, braking, checking your blind spot, and most importantly, being aware of what other drivers may or may not do. You have to tune your awareness antennae to sensitive mode if you're to become aware that there's a problem.

The grown up way of setting objectives includes a problem-assessment or problem-anticipation section. An excellent way to uncover possible hidden problems is to review the objective you've set by asking, "What's going to trip us up?" By identifying the possibilities now, you can plan how you're going to prevent delays, keep costs under control, and hit your objective successfully and on time.

Put your pessimist hat on and ask yourself…

- What could go wrong? What might the impact be?
- What areas do you need to keep an eye on, just in case?
- What could be catastrophic or just an irritant?
- What can you mitigate?

For example, if you're manufacturing a product which has several components supplied by different suppliers, what will happen if one supplier has a flood at their factory and can't supply your components? You might consider holding extra stock or sourcing an alternative supplier. Do you know who else will be able to supply what you need when you need it? A little work now can save lots of time later. You might even find a better alternative supplier that saves you money or time.

Problems crop up all over the place and they may not be in your control, as the supplier example shows. They're hard enough to spot within your own business, never mind externally. They don't always wave a pirate flag to let you know where they're lurking. You have to go looking for the problems. Walk around the premises; see what's happening. Talk to customers: what do they really think of your business? What can you learn from your suppliers? What's happening in the wider world? New competitors, new products, new distribution channels, new technology –

any of these could be a problem for you in the future. Legal changes can have a big impact, positive or negative, so keep your ear to the ground. The KPI dashboard you created in the last chapter is a great early-warning system, as is the market you operate in, what your competitors are doing, and how your customers are reacting to them and to you.

Grown-Up Businesses actively seek out problems. More often than not, they can turn problems into opportunities. Kodak's big mistake when they discovered digital pictures was to try to bury the technology, so they could keep selling rolls of film. If they'd embraced the new technology, they could have been at the forefront of a new industry, instead of struggling to survive.

At this precise moment, it may seem easier to ignore the problem, but eventually you will have to deal with it. You can't keep going round and round in circles – stalking the problem, and then leaving it on the too difficult pile. Your aim is to avoid firefighting – to stop whacking moles!

Frances and The Clipper NoteBook Company

It's six weeks until Mother's Day and sales are way down on last year for the same period. Sales have been flying since Mother's Day last year, when she seemed to hit a tipping point. Now it appears that tipping point was just a mirage. Something just isn't right. Why aren't sales orders in line with the target? What's going on?

- ⮌ Give yourself plenty of thinking time and ask yourself "what if" questions.
- ⮌ Make time regularly to step back and look at your business as if you are a stranger to it. Ask questions of everyone. Note down what you discover that needs your attention.
- ⮌ Think like a customer. How would you feel if you were a customer of your company? If you find that hard, engage a mystery shopping expert who can test, review, and report back to you.
- ⮌ Now go away and let your subconscious get to work on the dilemma.
- ⮌ Many people don't ask the question because they're frightened to hear the answer. Put that fear aside: if you don't ask the question, you won't find out what's wrong and you'll never be able to solve it.

2. Analyse - Uncover the facts

Uncovering the real problem is a bit like tackling an iceberg: only a small percentage is visible, but there's a lot happening below the surface. It's the same regardless of the problem you're trying to uncover.

Getting to the root cause of the problem is critical, so keep digging until you get there. It takes time. Be careful not to knee-jerk react when you uncover what appears to be the problem; keep looking. What you've found might just be another symptom and not the real problem.

There are only six questions to ask and you'll need to repeat them again and again. They are Rudyard Kipling's six best friends: *who, what, when, where, why,* and *how*. None of these questions will give you a yes or no answer; they demand more thought, explanation, and discovery. Remember your children asking *why, why* and *but why* until you were completely out of explanations? They were only using the questions to discover something from each angle. Uncovering the real problem is no different. Keep asking questions and analysing. Don't just ask one person: cast your net wide; get as much input and intelligence as you can before you test whether you've uncovered the real problem.

Three more questions you can ask are slight adaptations to the six best friends. They are *what if..., who cares,* and *so what*.

Many of you will be concerned about opening a can of worms. You probably will, but once you've opened it, don't jam the lid back on. You'll only have to face the worms again soon.

As you start to uncover the facts, you might find that it's not just one problem. It may be a combination of problems or issues. In that case, accurately defining each element is the first step to solving it.

Frances and The Clipper NoteBook Company

Frances knew that she had to tackle this problem head on and uncover what was really going on. She had a deadline – Mother's Day, her biggest selling opportunity for the entire year, would be over in six weeks. She set about finding out using the six questions *who, what, when, where, why,* and *how.*

Sales to wholesalers and major retailers were fine, but Frances put in a call to a couple of buyers. Their sales were as expected, although they did feel that Mother's Day was a little slow so far, probably because it came hot on the heels of Easter this year. So perhaps not an issue.

Frances hadn't spotted any new "copy cats" on the market, just the usual competition from the beautiful Paperblanks.

The KPI dashboard showed that sales had dropped since the end of January (it was now the end of February), but strangely, returns had increased over the same period. Could the fall in sales be a production or quality issue?

Finally, Frances reviewed the marketing campaign and promotions that were in place. She was really happy with them – they said the right things and the promotions were spot on. It was beginning to feel like a production problem.

➲ Keep the six questions on the tip of your tongue and use them frequently.

3. Identity - What's the real problem?

Once you think you've found the real problem, check and then double-check that you've got to the root cause and found all the problems. Detective work is crucial. You need to pull in information from a variety of sources. The more widely you look at the problem, the better your analysis will be. It's like peeling an onion: you have to get off all the layers.

What is your thought process when the car won't start? I'm guessing that you run through a checklist in your head: petrol, battery, oil, and so on. Uncovering the real problem in a business is no different. You need a checklist and a process to help you find out everything. You can't skip this step – you have to gather all the facts (hard data) and intelligence (soft data), and review them, then you'll have a much better chance of making the very best decision.

Don't get "paralysis through analysis", though: at some point, you have to do something. You can't afford to get stuck in this circle for too long; time is money. Just make sure that you are as thorough as you can be.

Frances and The Clipper NoteBook Company

With her investigations in full swing, Frances was digging a bit more. She found the boxes of returns from customers and was surprised to see the quality of the ones that had been returned. They had been well used and obviously loved, and they were last year's designs. It didn't seem to be a current production problem then. But what? She asked the questions again.

- Why were they coming back?
- What was her company doing with them when they came back?
- Were they justified returns?
- How many replacements had we sent out?
- Why hadn't anyone checked with her when they'd been sent back?
- Who was in charge of returns?

Frances discovered that for every returned notebook, her team had sent out a brand new one to replace it – expensive. But why had it suddenly happened?

⊃ Review your KPIs, talk to employees, customers, and suppliers, seek external views, benchmark yourself, quiz trade associations, and pair up with a local business that isn't in your competitive space to compare notes.

⊃ Soft data is just as important as hard data: people's feelings, thoughts, beliefs, perceptions and reactions are gold dust. Collect those, too.

4. Review - Step back, see more

The next three skills focus on choice: be sure you choose the best option. No one has the monopoly on a good idea, so remember that solutions can come from unexpected quarters. All options are valid at the start; don't rule them out too early. Solving the real and identified problem means viewing the business from different perspectives, employing logical and creative skills, and asking the right questions.

Mull over the possible solutions; sleep on them. Mix up facts and feelings; see what develops. Act like a stranger: take an outside and elevated view. Ask yourself, "If I weren't involved in this business, what would I see?"

We all have this skill. We're great at telling other people what's wrong or how they could do something better, a bit like the back-seat driver does! You just need to apply the same skill to your own business.

We need both logical and creative skills to solve problems effectively. Many problems can be solved by using gradual, systematic, and logical reasoning. In this scenario, you gather all the data, fit it together, and apply logic. Then you test the logic using the standard trial-and-error method. When logic doesn't work first time, you try another logical idea, until you find the right one. But this takes time, something you might not have.

Creative problem solving requires innovation, imagination, curiosity, insight, intuition, inspiration, and free or blue-sky thinking. Creativity isn't always creating something completely new – often, it's taking an existing idea and applying creative thought to turn that into a better idea.

Search out other people's ideas: let your curiosity lead you to discover ideas. A great source of inspiration is viewing what other non-related industries do and how you can adapt that to make big changes in your own company.

A well-run brainstorming session is a great way to develop creative solutions. Don't just restrict the thoughts to the senior team. Get a range of people involved, especially those who are mavericks or who defy convention; they are usually the ones who deliver creative solutions for you. And remember: brainstorming individually then combining ideas produces more ideas and more creative ideas, while a group working together is best at selecting ideas.

If you can't see the wood for the trees, how can you be confident that you have a good overview of the situation? Try these three perspectives to help you: the helicopter, the shark, and the glass bowl.

The helicopter

Imagine you're in a helicopter hovering over your company. What do you see when you look in from above? This view should make you think more widely and broadly about your business. You should see the impact on your customers and suppliers – in fact, anyone that your business touches. It will also help you to consider what's going on in the wider world that could impact your ability to define and then solve the problem.

The shark

Sometimes you need to get down and dirty, right into the detail. There have been many business television programmes where the CEOs have gone to work on the shop floor for a week. I'm always amazed when CEOs are able to do this by going undercover; surely every employee knows who the CEO is? If you don't spend time on the front line, you won't have any chance of identifying the problems early enough.

This is my shark tactic: look up from under the business. As you look up, what do you see?

The glass bowl

The helicopter and the shark are the up and down views, but what about the sideways view? Visualise yourself putting your entire company into a glass bowl. What do you see when you look in from outside? Again, act as a stranger: what would you see differently?

New recruits are a great source of intelligence and observation, as they bring that outsider view. On the Friday afternoon after they start, ask the new recruit what they think of the company, what's odd or strange, what is great and what's wrong. Trust me, you'll learn lots.

Frances and The Clipper NoteBook Company

In the early days of The Clipper NoteBook Company, Frances had been very keen to make sure that her early customers always had exactly what they needed, so that these customers would become her sales team. She also knew that many of her notebooks would be bought as presents. She wanted everyone to love the one they were given, but just in case they didn't like the design their friend had chosen, she offered a free swap service.

This was a great promotional tool in the early days, but unworkable now. It seemed that as long as the notebook had The Clipper NoteBook Company tab logo inside the back cover, it could be replaced. The chap handling the returns just looked for the tab and sent out the one they'd requested. That's what he'd been told to do, so he did it.

The problem was not actually a lack of sales: it's that they were giving free replacements. "Surely we don't still offer our free swap service?" asked Frances. The promotion had been taken off the website. She had two questions:

- Why were customers still sending their old ones back, expecting to be sent a new one?
- Why was the company still sending out free notebooks?

Firstly, it turned out that the terms and conditions had not been changed, despite a request from Frances. Actually, they were changed, but not to the right version. An old version was posted by mistake, which still had the free swap included. Secondly, no one had told the returns chap that the process had changed. So, for the last three months, since the change of terms and conditions, The Clipper NoteBook Company had been sending out free replacements. Canny daughters had been sending back their own notebooks for a replacement to give to their mum on Mother's Day and then they would probably send their mum's back to get a replacement for themselves. It was time to put a stop to it and see how much it had cost the company.

➲ Try using the helicopter, shark, and glass bowl tactics.

➲ Go back to the shop floor every now and then to see what's different. Try to act as a stranger: keep your eyes and ears open to what's actually happening and consider what a stranger might comment on.

➲ Identify team members who can be creative and nurture their skills by using them to help you.

5. Decide - Choose the best one

This is the middle of the process. Make the wrong decision here and it could be expensive. Make the right decision and you're on the road to success. You've applied your logical and creative skills, and looked at it from the three perspectives. You'll be starting to think about prioritising the best option.

You know the problem is clearly and accurately identified and expressed, through your analysis and because you've identified some options by "being a stranger". Now you need to assess the options by rating each one. For each option you'll consider…

- cost of implementation and the return on that investment
- benefits, to customers first, then to your bottom line
- timescales to implement it and then to see the return
- resources, people and money certainly and machinery a possibility
- impact on stakeholders, customers, employees, suppliers and the community

Once you have your scoring sheet, you can rank the options and make your choice. Throughout this process, don't allow your personal favourites to dictate what you choose or how you rate it. Make an informed decision.

Sometimes, when you get to your preferred option, you can't go with it. For example, you might discover it'll cost much more than you originally thought. Creative problem solving needs to kick in again. There's always another way of doing something if you have to; ask any inventor!

When you identify your plan A, make sure you've also identified a plan B and plan C, just in case plan A doesn't come to fruition.

Frances and The Clipper NoteBook Company

No one had spotted the error in the terms and conditions. Poor communication had compounded the problem: Frances had no idea how many returns they were getting. At least she knew what the problem was now. It wasn't poor sales at all. The root cause was three-fold:

- failure to upload the correct version of the terms and conditions
- failure to change and update the process for dealing with a return
- failure to communicate to the team or to train them in the new procedures

In this case, making the decision on corrective action was easy: correctly implement what should have been done before. But that was not all. Frances felt that there should be some further actions, too, to make sure these problems didn't arise again.

➲ Don't rush the decision-making, but don't dilly-dally either.
➲ Ask yourself the six questions, *who, what, when, where, why,* and *how* so that you investigate each option thoroughly.

6. Prescribe - Who does what and when

Having made your decision, you now need to define the plan. The six-best-friends questions are still a good place to start:

- *What* has to be done?
- *Who* is going to do what?
- *When* does it need to happen and when will it be completed?
- *Where* are the changes and corrections going to be made?
- *Why* are we doing this? Put everything in context, especially when you're communicating to staff, customers, suppliers, and so on.
- *How* are we going to make the changes?

Set a clear vision and objective for the plan, including the timescales, budget, and resources you'll need. What will success look like? Get the plan down on paper, clear and concise, with time deadlines. Remember to include checkpoints throughout the plan to make sure you are on track. If plan A doesn't work, you might need to switch to plan B. Now assign responsibilities, get everyone pointing in the same direction, and direct (don't do) the implementation of the plan.

Frances and The Clipper NoteBook Company

Doing nothing was not an option; the company would go bust! Frances set about prescribing what needed to be done, by whom, by when, and how it was to be done.

- The correct terms and conditions were uploaded.
- The process for updating the website terms and conditions was updated to include a second person checking that the correct version had been uploaded.
- The returns process was rewritten and the team retrained.
- The KPIs dashboard was updated to include reporting on returns.

Frances also stipulated further steps:

- Everyone who'd taken advantage of the free swap service would receive a letter saying that this service would no longer be available, but that she hoped that her customers enjoyed their new Clipper NoteBook. She also included a discount voucher for them to use against their next Clipper Notebook purchase.
- She asked marketing to start a social media campaign to find the most loved Clipper NoteBook. This would engage her target audience and also provide good PR stories for the future.
- All products returned would be followed up directly with the customer by phone to find out what the problem was, both to solve it quickly and to alert Frances to the reasons.

Frances was annoyed with her team for not thinking or acting on something so obvious, but mostly with her own complacency. She'd learnt a very expensive lesson.

➲ You won't always need a Gantt chart, MS Project plan or a Prince2 trained project manager; so only use them when necessary.

➲ In its simplest form, write a clear written declaration of what has to be done, *why*, by *whom*, by *when*, *where* and *how*. This is enough for most tasks; the important part is to get on and do it!

7. Systematise - It starts with you

This skill is all about getting it done. Somebody has to drive it through to completion, check that it works as it should do, and tick it off the list. That person is you: you're the boss. You can't be erratic, abdicate responsibility, or lose interest – if you do, so will everyone else, and then nothing will improve! Although you're not directly delivering the plan, the project team will be relying on your problem-solving skills and leadership to ensure the plan is completed smoothly and successfully.

We've learnt how essential systematising is, so for every change you make you'll need to update your system documents, communicate those changes, train your team, and start measuring again.

Frances and The Clipper NoteBook Company

Frances had prescribed what needed to be done to solve the problem now and to make sure that it never happened again. By far the biggest piece of work was to make sure that the processes were updated and tested to make sure they worked. While she had identified how the problem was caused in the first place – the wrong terms and conditions were posted on the website – she had to be careful not to replicate the problem when the transition period was over. The terms and conditions would need changing again in the future, so the process needed a robust testing element too.

Everyone knew how Frances felt about the problem and what it might have led to. They also felt bad about it and so the entire team pulled together to correct the process. They had had a front-row seat at the problem party and didn't want to be there again. Systematisation was the new buzz word for The Clipper NoteBook Company.

⮑ Lead by example, stay focused, and drive the implementation through the checkpoints. Don't be afraid to adjust strategy or focus if it's not working correctly.

8. Commit - Tough it out

Even when we actively seek to solve the problem, there are times when the idea just doesn't work. So tough it out, get back to the drawing board, and ask yourself whether plan B or C are still viable. If not, work through the steps again, this time learning from your mistakes.

To complete the task and get to a resolution takes commitment, lots of it. You'll encounter barriers, obstacles, and some seemingly insurmountable challenges along the way. Each one will test people's commitment. It would be so easy, sometimes, to let the pressure drop, to slack off, to do nothing, or to dump it on the "I'll do it later" pile. But if you do, you'll end up revisiting this same problem sometime soon. Bite the bullet and do it now.

You must gain commitment from everyone, directly involved or not, at the start, and continually reinforce it throughout the project. The team will want to do their best and your commitment is to support them in whatever way necessary.

Frances and The Clipper NoteBook Company

Issuing replacements for free had been a costly problem, one which Frances could not and would not ignore. Her commitment was total; her baby was in real trouble; urgent attention was needed. She knew it was her fault and she personally helped design and implement the changes.

⮑ Retain a clear vision of what success is, in your head. What's it going to be like knowing that you'll never have to deal with that problem ever again?

9. Lead - Finish it

Finally, you're carrying out the plan and solving the problem. Keep hold of your vision of your end goal and what a positive change its successful conclusion will have on everyone. Keep going until the job is done; no half measures are allowed here. Remember: finished means *finished*, not "almost done" or "I'll do that bit later." This is Solzhenitsyn's realm of the last inch.

It's not all over when the implementation is complete. You need checkpoints to make sure that the changes you've made have really and truly solved the problem. Continual monitoring and measurement will prove whether or not it's been a success and will also tell you if there are other aspects that need addressing.

How good do you feel knowing that the problem has been solved? It might have been a painful process, but certainly worth the effort. Just think how much money, time, effort, and stress you'll be saving from now on, by not revisiting the same problem again.

Having recognised how damaging problems are to the business, it's time to search out some more problems and solve them, now and forever. It's time to move from being a boss that firefights all the time to someone who focuses on fire prevention.

Frances and The Clipper NoteBook Company

After the free swap problem, Frances was much more aware and was often seen on the shop floor, checking all sorts of processes – and, of course, the very few returns that they have now.

➲ Don't ignore those post-project checkpoints and make sure that you have a future review date scheduled to check whether or not anything else can be done to improve the process.

Now that you have completed the nine-step process with your team, ask yourself…

➲ Do your team understand how important problem solving is and the damage an ignored problem can do to a business?
➲ What are your current business goals? Are you on track to hit or exceed them? Have you been knocked off track by a problem?
➲ Could you have foreseen this problem if you'd taken the time to think about possible problems?
➲ When did you last review your complaints log to see how many recurring themes there are? This is a great place to start solving problems.

Chapter 10

Opportunity Knocks

Welcome to your Grown-Up Business. It's running like a well-oiled machine. Do you want to sell it or grow it even more? It's decision time. Opportunities will be landing in your lap without much effort, but do you want to take advantage of them or not? Perhaps it's time to make your own opportunities.

In this last chapter, we're going to review the work we have done so far, keeping the focus on your customers and increasing those happy faces. We'll consider the opportunities that you now have in front of you and whether or not it's time to sell. Finally, we'll redo the spider chart from chapter one, so that you can see how you've moved the business forward and start celebrating.

Your Grown-Up Business is...

Let's look back at the Growing up Business Model and establish how you have progressed through the growing pains of each stage of development.

The Growing-Up business model

Stage	Mode	Focus	Growth %	Fun Index
Mature	Momentum	Opportunity	64	☺☺☺
Family	Direction	Leadership	32	☺☺
Young Adult	Activity	Implementation	16	☺
Teenager	Strategy	Commitment	8	☺
Early Years	Decision	Discovery	4	☹
Birth	Survival	Measurement	0	☹☹
Pregnancy	Research	Planning	0	☹☹☹

You won't have completed the transformation yet – that will take some time – but you're making great progress. In many respects, you never stop growing up; there's always something new to learn! Even moving up one level is a significant change in your business. Keep your eye on the next level as you methodically complete the actions at each stage.

It's probably been tough at times and not everything will have gone smoothly, but as we saw with Frances from The Clipper NoteBook Company, you can overcome the obstacles and put the right systems in place, and success will come.

You'll see that your company is turning into a Grown-Up Business. It's more effective, efficient, profitable, consistent, confident, rewarding and engaged.

Effective

Your systems are more effective than they were at delivering the product or service to your standards. Effectiveness is about your ability to deliver your vision consistently every time and about being successful in producing the result you want. "Effective leadership is putting first things first. Effective management is discipline, carrying it out," writes Stephen Covey in *The 7 Habits of Highly Effective People*. When you are more effective, you produce more, sell more, and make more money.

Efficient

Efficiency is an equally important attribute in any Grown-Up Business. The business recognises that its inputs, its resources, are scarce – whether that's time, money, energy, effort, or raw materials, they are all limited. So it makes commercial sense to try to use them as efficiently as possible, while maintaining your output. Being efficient simply means reducing the amount of wasted inputs, but don't mistake efficient for fast. Efficiency is about doing it *right* first time.

Consistent

A Grown-Up Business is easily recognisable because it is consistently consistent. Your customers receive the same experience, value, and service every time they engage with you and they keep on engaging, buying more and more. They also recommend you to more and more people, more and more often. Suppliers love working with you and employees love working for you. Your attention to detail in designing systems that give the customer, supplier, investor, and employee the best and consistent experience possible is what you've been working towards. Tom Landry, the celebrated American football player and coach, said, "The secret to winning is constant, consistent management." It's the same in business.

Confident

Joe Namath said, "When you have confidence, you can have a lot of fun. And when you have fun, you can do amazing things." A confident Grown-Up Business is not arrogant. It has earned the confidence of its customers by building a set of products and services that they are confident buying repeatedly. Its suppliers are confident that the company will pay on time and work in partnership with them. You are confident that you know your market, your products, your customers, and your staff, because you've taken the time to fully understand them. As your confidence grows, your decision-making improves and that's infectious too. Now you confidently plan the future.

Profitable

A Grown-Up Business is focused on the bottom line. Without profit, what's the point? You understand your margins and which products deliver the most profit. You've removed waste and duplication from the business, saving more money. You're diligent about retaining customers and ensuring that repeat purchases increase. Your team knows that when they spend money, they're spending your money, and are careful.

Engaged

Anne M Mulcahy, the former chairperson and CEO of the Xerox Corporation said, "Employees who believe that management is concerned about them as a whole person, not just an employee, are more productive, more satisfied, more fulfilled. Satisfied employees means satisfied customers, which leads to profitability."

Engaged employees care about what they do and they're proud to give customers the best experience every time. They understand the *what* and the *why* of your vision and work hard to help you achieve it. Everything they do is focused on the customers. This results in engaged customers buying more, creating future growth. As Michael Le Boeuf put it, "A satisfied customer is the best business strategy of all."

Rewarding

Wow, how much better is life now that you are becoming a Grown-Up Business? You feel more fulfilled and you're reaping the rewards of all that hard work. It's been tough, but so rewarding too. You choose how you spend your time, you might even decide to sell the company, but it's now so much fun running the business that you might not – it's your choice.

Customer-centric

Without customers, you don't have a business. Without attracting more new customers, you don't have a growing business. But having lots of customers who never repeat-purchase is a disaster. All that hard work attracting new customers only to totally underwhelm them so that they never buy again is such a waste. That's not a sign of a profitable, reliable, trustworthy, or sustainable business and certainly not a Grown-Up Business.

There are so few truly Grown-Up Businesses, but one aspect they all focus on above everything else is the customer. The customer determines everything they do: the products and services they sell, the distribution channel, the service, the aftercare, and the price. One of Amazon's corporate values is customer obsession.

Why is a customer centric organisation more grown up?

- It only makes the things their customers really want and will pay for.
- Customers enjoy the purchasing experience and feel valued, so they buy again.
- Your existing customers will sell for you, buying more themselves but also "selling you" to family and friends.
- They proactively make suggestions for product improvements, changes, and enhancements. It's easy to get valuable feedback, proactive and constructive rather than critical and destructive.
- They will happily pay to test new products: they are your reliable beta testers.

By keeping the customer at the very heart of your company and your focus on doing everything to ensure a consistent customer experience, you'll see sales increase. As sales momentum builds, you see the tipping point appear on the horizon. The tipping point, according to Malcolm Gladwell in his book of the same name, is "that magic moment when ideas, trends and social behaviour cross a threshold, tips, and spreads like wildfire."

The Grown-Up Business doesn't risk upsetting or disappointing customers. It works hard to identify the problems before they happen so a customer never has cause to complain. Remember, good news is rarely shared, but bad news spreads like wildfire.

At The Ambrette, the customer is the most important person. Yes, the food must be fantastic but it has to be what the customer wants and will pay for. One aspect that the chef and owner Dev Biswal does very well is taster events. They're usually on a Monday night and he invites a selected audience from his customer database to sample his new menu ideas for a set price. It costs the diner much less than usual. Dev prepares the dishes, the same for everyone, and then asks his diners to give feedback for every dish (appearance, taste, portion size) and he asks them to price the dish too.

The diners feel engaged and thrilled when a dish they tasted and commented on hits the menu. Dev's attention to detail, and his willingness to ask customers what they think and to act on criticism, has seen The Ambrette grow and open its third restaurant in as many years.

- ↻ Would you buy from you?
- ↻ What little changes would you personally suggest if you'd been a customer? Better still, why not mystery-shop your company?
- ↻ Would you recommend the last five businesses that you've used?
- ↻ When was the last time you asked customers what they think of your company? Take a little time to do this with some customers and understand what is really happening at the coal face.

Happy faces

When people smile at you, you naturally smile back; it's infectious. Sadly, so is gloom. Living and working with miserable, fed-up, demotivated people infects you with the same miserable feeling. Surrounding yourself with happy, smiling, positive people is so much better and that's when the 2 + 2 = 5 magic happens. Positive people bring out the best in each other, energy levels increase, problems are solved, solutions are developed, and the business grows.

Grown-Up Businesses naturally attract happy people – and they make their people happy. Talented people want to work with you; they want to engage with the brand. Fulfilled employees contribute more and stay longer. Happy customers are great to work with, pay on time, value what you do, and are nice to do business with. Satisfied customers buy more for longer. Investors are easier to find and it's easier to persuade them to invest. Happy suppliers give you great service and super credit terms too. They also bend over backwards to help bring opportunities to your door.

By now your business will have moved through some of the Growing-Up stages. Non-productive and negative employees will have been replaced by proactive, positive people, all eager to please. Talented employees can be more expensive, but they're worth the extra if they're the right fit. They'll quickly understand your vision and the standards you set. Your work house-rules will be universally adopted.

Now the business is growing up, you have higher productivity, lower sickness, louder laughter, less stress, better ideas, and improved consistency, all delivering significant cost savings and improved profit. Not only do you attract good people, but you retain your great team too. Growth starts to accelerate as your business moves through Young Adult into Family and on to Maturity.

Your suppliers, investors (even the bank manager with money to offer you), employees, and of course customers are all queuing up to do business with you, help you, make you offers, suggest things, share connections, open doors, recommend you, and so on. All the things you worked so hard for now seem to happen as if by magic. Why? Because people want to be associated with a successful Grown-Up Business. Instead of your having to tempt a celebrity to be the face of your brand, they will be offering to work for you. They also want to be associated with successful brands.

If you've ever been to Bicester Village, you'll understand what I'm talking about. Bicester Village is a retail destination with a difference. It's full of outlet stores, but from the top end of the market. It's high class, desirable, and expensive; everything about it is targeted at its specific market.

Its vision is clear; the product, service, and customer experience are paramount. Its set of standards, brand manifesto, and work house-rules are all focused on the customer experience. Every member of staff – and I mean everyone – has a smile on their face.

Scratch under the surface and you'll see how deep it runs. Whichever retail unit you're in, you're asked if you are enjoying your day *at Bicester Village* – not at the shop you're in, Hobbs, Gucci, Prada or Mulberry.

Unlike other retail destinations, Bicester Village is fully occupied, with no vacant shops. Why? Bicester is a successful Grown-Up Business that people want to be part of or associated with. I bet Bicester can select who they have in their retail units and the rents they pay. Other shopping centres are pleased just to be occupied.

- ➲ What makes your business attractive to…
  1 employees?
  2 suppliers?
  3 customers?
  4 investors?
- ➲ Are you actively seeking talented people to join your organisation? Do you need to make your business even more attractive to get the talent?
- ➲ When was the last time an employee resigned? What reasons did they give?
- ➲ When was the last time you lost a supplier or a customer? Did you find out why they left you?

Time to take advantage

Whether or not you intend to sell your venture, keep the business on track and clearly focused on its goals in the meantime. Don't let anything slip just because you might be thinking of selling.

From the Birth of your business and its initial survival, you've measured everything in your business, to discover what's happening and make better decisions. You've developed your strategy and committed to delivering it, then focused on the implementation and increased activity, to reach the Young Adult stage. As you approach the Family stage, your focus turns to leadership, which enables you to develop direction. All this effort leads into momentum and rhythm, which means that you can focus on maximising opportunities.

Once you can lift your head up and look around you, you'll be able to spot more opportunities. Doing something different and finding some clear head space and thinking time will help you to identify even more opportunities.

1   You can look for opportunities
Here you'll need your clear head space, thinking time, and time away from the business – a holiday, perhaps? Read, research, and think about options.

2   You will be offered opportunities
They'll be offered to you because you head up a successful business with which people want to be associated. You've become the go-to person, recognised within your industry as a good person to do business with. You're probably a key person of influence. You're presented with opportunities – many more than you could imagine, although many you'll decide that you don't want.

3   You can make opportunities happen
As the business is running smoothly, doing exactly what it should be doing, you'll have time to assess whether or not an opportunity is a good one for you and the business. If so, then you'll have time to make it happen.

4   You can meet new people
New people are always a great source of new ideas, new perspectives, and new opportunities. You'll be able to make even more connections than

before, find chances to explore new partnerships, and make better, more influential connections than when you started.

5   You have money to invest in opportunities
Now your Grown-Up Business is delivering grown-up profits and you'll be earning rewards, both you personally and the business will have money to invest. You'll also have time to invest as well as money.

6   You can test out your theories
Up to this point, you'll have had ideas and thoughts of what you might have wanted to do, but you were poor in time and money. Now that's changing, it's time to resurrect your own theories and make them reality.

- Dedicate some thinking time. As a starting point, pull out all those ideas you had which you filed away for a later date.
- Book a holiday or do something that you've always wanted to do. Get some clear head space and let your mind wander.
- Start learning again: it's time to catch up on all the reading you've missed.
- Write down who you would like to meet and why.
- Start planning out your business future. Try a mind mapping exercise and focus on *who* you want to work with, *what* you want to do, *when* you are going to do it, *why* you want to do it, *where* you would like to do it, and *how*.

Stay or go?

Perhaps one of the biggest decisions approaching you is whether you should sell your company or not. Let me tell you, it's hard to make that final decision until the money is actually on the table.

What a Grown-Up Business is expert at doing, though, is always being ready to sell. It doesn't mean that you're going to sell, but if you're ready when that fantastic offer arrives, so much the better.

Deciding whether or not to sell may be an easy decision for some. One of my clients had this as their number-one objective when they launched their business. Everything we did was geared to the ultimate sale and they were approached ahead of the target date with a fantastic offer. Their "sale pack" was ready, which reduced the time frame for the sale.

You have several options:

1   Keep growing the business
You might decide that you have unfinished business, have more to achieve, or you're too young to retire.

2   Diversify
Your business is running like clockwork, but you want another challenge. You could add another division, launch a new product, or enter new markets. You could also diversify your interests by becoming a non-executive director in another company or starting a foundation or charity work. For example, one of my clients teaches rowing to schoolkids two afternoons a week, because he can and because he wants to.

3   Retirement
For many business owners, retirement is totally overrated. I've tried it twice and lasted three months each time. I'm much happier with Tim Ferris's approach of mini retirements. Tim's book, *The 4-Hour Work Week*, is one of my recommended reads, especially the mini-retirement section.

4   Pass on to the next generation

5   Exit
This could be a full or partial exit, depending on your goals. If you are going to sell the entire company, consider retaining (if you can) 1 to 2%. Wouldn't you want to keep a small shareholding in something successful that you've built?

There are many escape options and exit strategies for business owners, whether planned or not. Let's look at how you might want, or have to, exit the business, and then at what you need in place to sell your business.

1. The planned exit

You've built your business and you know how you are going to exit. You have planned the exit; you're in control. Your options include…

- selling your business
  - o   to your employees
  - o   to another company

- o   to investors
- o   on the open market
- passing your business on to the next generation
- IPO (initial public offering) taking the business public
- liquidating the business

2. The unplanned exit

Not every exit can be planned: some are forced, which is why it is so important to always be ready to sell. It could be a nasty event, one of the three Ds: death, divorce, or disability. It could be imminent insolvency or bankruptcy that forces the exit, perhaps you're voted out, or the business has a too-good-to-miss offer for the company. A fellow shareholder might want to sell up, so the terms of your shareholder agreement mean that the sale must proceed, although you should get first refusal!

Sell your business like a house

One piece of advice from BCMS Ltd (www.bcmscorporate.com) that I heard many years ago (and which in fact applies to selling almost anything) is this: don't put a price tag on it. The minute you do, you have set the top price you'll get. You've also given the buyer a reason to reduce the price with every little niggle or problem they find with the product. And your business is just a product to a buyer!

So what do you need in place to sell? You need to treat selling your business as you would a house.

1   It has to be attractive from the outside
People perceive (because they can't know for sure) that you're making lots of money and that you have great customers, patents, systems, and so on, in place. You're a company to watch, perhaps one that's already causing competitors concern.

2   It's not going to fall down
It's financially secure, no laws have been broken, it isn't hiding anything, and it wasn't built on dodgy foundations. The business is in the right sector, area, or industry for them. The paperwork is in order. Ownership is straightforward, funding is in place, contracts and licences are legally drawn up, and the database has been tested. There are no claims or

disputes that might be a problem. Searches are satisfactory. Skeletons have been brought out of the closet and willingly shared through negotiations or have been uncovered by the buyer and the price has gone down.

3 It has potential

It may not be exactly what the buyer is looking for, but it has the potential to be a great purchase or investment. There are opportunities, it has a customer database that could be fantastic, a good stream of new products or possible patents in the pipeline, it's a recognised brand, and so on.

4 It can be improved

Many buyers are looking for a business that they can add value to. It might be linking it with something they already have, spotting a great opportunity to remove significant costs in the business, or making a big leap forward in what is supplied. Some buyers want something that isn't perfect for a good price, but others are willing to pay extra for the readymade solution.

5 It doesn't need much work and everything is in working order

It all works really well. They won't need to redecorate; they can just move in and enjoy straight away. The systematisation is great, it works, and everything runs smoothly. The customer experience is good.

6 Great neighbours

This addition will fit very well into their existing business if they buy it. There are things that it has in common which make it attractive. Perhaps the customer base is perfect for the products the other company is selling. A bit like good neighbours, the businesses complement each other.

7 It's worth the money

What they're paying for it makes it great value to them. The price might not have suited other purchasers, but they can see the value in it. The purchase might have gone to a tendering process – they bid what they thought it was worth, but they secured the deal.

The Grown-Up Business's sales-ready pack

If you're selling a house, you'll have a short two-pager with the headlines that tempt a potential buyer. It's the same with your business. This must not include any commercially sensitive information – for example, don't list your top 10 clients; simply state that your clients include several household names and leave it at that. This is a public document and is given to anyone who expresses interest.

If they're interested, they'll approach you and sign an NDA (non-disclosure agreement) *before* you give them the full sales pack. At this stage, a Grown-Up Business will start its own due diligence on a potential buyer, to make sure they're serious and have sufficient funds available to complete the purchase.

This is what the full sales pack will contain.

1   Company Overview
When it was established and all the paperwork to prove it, its history, the business it is in, the markets in which it operates, its USPs, an overview of the employees and key staff members as well as the management team structure, any subsidiaries, dormant companies, the premises and major assets owned by the company, and any specific intellectual property owned by the company

2   Shareholding
Who owns what and how much they participate in the business, who the investors are, what's in the shareholder agreement (a Grown-Up Business will always have one of these – if you don't own 100% of your company and this is missing, then get one in place right now!), why you are selling the company, and whether you want a clean break, an earn-out, or to retain a small number of shares or a role in the future organisation

3   Products and services
What you sell, have sold, and hope to sell; details of patents, licences, design rights, trademarks, domains, and so on; any contractual agreements, distribution arrangements, exclusive deals, or long-term arrangements; details of market share, margins, and repeat-purchase cycles

4   Clients
Overview of major customers (say the top 10); number of customers, lost and existing; database strength and accuracy; export sales and contracted sales; reputation analysis

5 Overview of the Market
A high level PESTLE analysis of the macro-market, highlighting opportunities and threats

6 Financials
A complete set of figures for past three to five years as well as the business forecast for the next three years; details of debtor performance; financial KPIs, balance sheet, P&L and monthly management accounts

7 Legals
Copies of all contracts, statutory papers, insurance contracts, staff contracts, and so on

8 Skeletons
If there is anything in the company's history that might be a problem to a prospective purchaser, get it out in the open as early as possible. There is no point trying to hide something: you will be found out! Do not leave them as a bombshell that you drop at the last minute either – that's a surefire way to get the buyer to walk away from the table with their money!

Inevitably, you will exit the business at some point. Even if you have a date fixed in your plan to sell and retire, it might happen earlier. You might say that you are never selling and your children will take over, but if they don't want it, what then? The best laid plans of mice and men…

I was at grammar school when Margaret Thatcher became leader of the Conservative party. As it was an all-girls school, we had a special assembly and were told that we could be whatever we wanted to be, but we had to work hard to earn the choices that we could make in the future. If I didn't work hard to learn the violin, for instance, I wouldn't have the choice to become a concert violinist.

When you have a Grown-Up Business, you have choices: to sell or not. The challenge is just deciding whether or not now is the right time to sell.

➲ Set out your exit route, your plan A – but also have a plan B, C, and D.
➲ What is your emergency exit route should something go terribly wrong with your personal life? Map out that exit route too.

○ Start working on your sales pack – this is something your accountant should be able to help you with.

○ Research how to sell your business. There are a number of companies providing free seminars and guides that will help you to get everything in order.

> 1 BCMS's half-day free Sell Your Business seminar is packed with information and they're not pushy. More information can be found at www.bcmscorporate.com.
>
> 2 Your accountant will be able to help you, but the minute he or she mentions putting it up for sale at £xx, walk away. Find someone who will help you sell the business for the best possible price, not the accountant's paper valuation. I was once told by a chartered accountant that there are at least 14 different ways to value a business and each one throws up a different number!
>
> 3 Talk to other business owners who've sold their business, ask them to talk you through the process, and find out who they used as their advisers. If they were selling another business, would they use the same advisors?

The Spider Chart

Let's take another look at your business, using the same chart we used at the start of the book. Again, mark yourself out of 10 for each of the 8 questions.

> 1 How well is your business growing?
>
> 2 How well are you supported, by your team and by your own advisors?
>
> 3 How clear are the guidelines for your business – customer service standards, team values and behaviours, and brand statement?
>
> 4 According to your cash flow forecast, how healthy does the next three months' trading look? How often do you review how your business operates, where you could make changes to either save or make more money?
>
> 5 How effective are the processes and systems in your business? Do they run smoothly and are they written down? When did you last review or improve them?
>
> 6 How often do you review your targets, business forecast, and performance? Do you have a current forecast in place?

7 How many problems have you dealt with this week – did you solve them permanently or will they pop up again?

8 How often do you want to kick yourself because you let a great opportunity slip through your fingers?

Put the scores onto the chart below and join the scores together to look like a spider's web. Now dig out the spider chart that you prepared in chapter 1 and compare them.

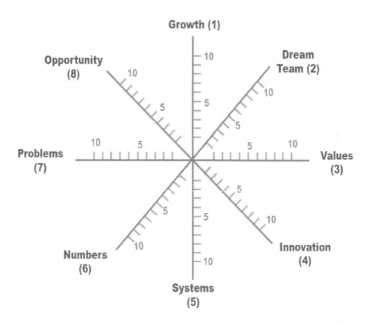

Becoming a Grown-Up Business will always be a testing journey; you'll never seem to reach the end. But it's vital that you stop and smell the roses, sniff the coffee, taste the fruits of your labours! Whichever metaphor you use, put it into practice. Periods of intense work only work well when you have a break and recharge your batteries, ready for the next push.

Hitting a milestone or achieving an objective only becomes significant if you celebrate the achievement. Whatever you do, don't forget to celebrate: put "celebrate" into your plan now, because there won't be anyone else to give you a pat on the back – you'll have to instigate that one yourself!

The choice is yours

You can become a Grown-Up Business if you want to. Out in the world, there are many businesses who've actually decided to make only a few improvements to the way they operate. The majority, though, know they *should* do something, but they just don't get around to it. Your mission, should you decide to accept it, is to take what you've learnt and put it into practice. Your reward is to become one of the few genuinely Grown-Up Businesses.

If you've already found someone to help you through this, you'll be making significant progress by now. It's tough to do this on your own. If you have a business partner, you both need to agree what has to be done so you can support each other to deliver the solutions. Don't ever be afraid or nervous to ask for help: that's a sign of strength, not weakness.

As you work through the Growing-Up Business model, you'll have times when your motivation, enthusiasm, and energy levels fail you. When this happens, it's easy to get sucked back into your old habits. Here are some reminders for you – mantras, perhaps, or little phrases that you can use to get yourself back on track. Why not auto-schedule some to pop up in your calendar or post them on your desk, your wall planner, in fact anywhere you'll see them.

- Standing still is boring: let's move forward.
- Let's make good even better.
- Be consistently consistent.
- Solve the real problem now, once and for all.
- Make time for the important stuff.
- I can, we can, and we will.
- I'm not perfect, the business isn't perfect, so let's make it better.
- Growing Up is for life; keep the business growing up.

What now?

This isn't the end of the journey. It's the start of a new approach to running your business, one that will see you overtake the competition, make more money, have more fun, time, choices, and opportunities, and be more successful!

As a business coach, I know that this is where the hard work starts: putting the plans in place, doing the actions, and implementing them. So I've created some resources to help you.

Go to www.grownupbusiness.com/extras and you'll find a complete blank set of the How To worksheets for each chapter that you can use to work through the exercises. There are also three extra case studies following Frances at The Clipper NoteBook Company Ltd, which I have written for you. You can read or download them.

While you're on the extras page, you can also sign up for a regular dose of inspirational hints, tips, and motivational stories, which are delivered to your inbox each month in my Grown-Up Business Master Tips.

I've loved writing this book and seeing the positive impact that it's had on those who have read it. I'd love to know what you think about the book; so please take a minute to leave your reviews and comments either on the website where you bought your book or on my website. www.grownupbusiness.com/reviews.

I couldn't have written this book without all of the businesses that I've worked with. Just as they've learnt from me, I've learnt what they needed from them. It is their questions that form the basis of this book. I'd love to learn what's challenging you, your successes, your hints and tips, and the problems you're facing. Please do email me at shirley@grownupbusiness.com.

My goal for this book is to spread the word and share the passion, knowledge, and confidence so that you can grow your business. I want to help business owners to have a better work-life balance, to succeed. So if you've found the book valuable, you've learnt something, or just enjoyed the journey, then do share your thoughts with a tweet, G+ or a post.

I'm on Twitter @GrownUpBusiness and online at www.grownupbusiness.com. Just use #grownupbusiness and we'll get the conversation started.

Recommended Reading

18 Minutes: Find your Focus, Master Distraction and Get The Right Things Done by Peter Bregman

The Tipping Point by Malcolm Gladwell

The 4-Hour Work Week by Tim Ferris

Work The System, The Simple Mechanics of Making More and Working Less by Sam Carpenter

The E-Myth Revisited by Michael Gerber

How to Be a Productivity Ninja by Graham Alcott

The Pumpkin Plan and The Toilet Paper Entrepreneur by Mike Michalowicz

Rework, Change the Way You Work Forever by Jason Fried and David Heinemeier Hansson

Get a Grip and Traction by Gino Wickman and Mike Paton

The 7 Habits of Highly Effective People by Stephen Covey

Acknowledgements

At school I loved maths and disliked English immensely, although I was an avid reader. It was a few years into my career when someone told me I was good at copy. And there, I guess, is where my writing started.

Thanks to Gareth, who made me start blogging, to Mark, who suggested being an author, and to Megan, who skilfully took me from blogger to writer to author; my heartfelt thanks.

Throughout my career there have been people who have inspired me, who saw a spark in me, and who cultivated me; to Vi Godfrey, Debbie Gorski, and Denis Harper, thank you.

Both Paul Walsh and Phil Beavan deserve my thanks for their challenge, guidance, and help when I started my coaching journey. Every day I quote some of your wise words!

To Chris and all the team from Filament for your belief, expertise, direction, and deadlines! Pam, thank you for your red pen!

Without my coaching clients, this book would not have seen the light of day. The book is a tribute to all SME business owners who are brave enough to follow their dream, put some skin in the game, and know when to ask for help! It's fantastic to see your businesses take off and I feel that I work for many successful companies all at the same time.

Even a coach needs some help, so thanks to Trish, Sharon, Michael, Deb, Mark, Paul, Claire, Steve J, Jo, Emma, and Phil.

To Steve for your support and for being there, and finally to Mum, an inspiration to everyone; thank you!

Printed in Great Britain
by Amazon

80193609R00138